ATLAS OF
ANCIENT WORLDS

Author
Peter Chrisp

Consultant
Philip Parker

LONDON, NEW YORK,
MELBOURNE, MUNICH, AND DELHI

Project art editor Rebecca Painter
Senior art editor Jacqui Swan
Project editor Hazel Beynon
Additional editors Fran Jones, Andrea Mills
Senior editor Shaila Brown

Managing editor Linda Esposito
Managing art editor Diane Thistlethwaite
Publishing manager Andrew Macintyre
Category publisher Laura Buller

Picture researcher Sarah Hopper
DK picture library Myriam Megharbi, Emma Shepherd
Production controller Erika Pepe
Production editor Hitesh Patel
Jacket editor Mariza O'Keeffe
Jacket designer Akiko Kato
Jacket manager Sophia M Tampakopoulos Turner

Cartographer John Plumer
Illustrator Mark Longworth

First published in Great Britain in 2009 by
Dorling Kindersley Limited, 80 Strand, London WC2R 0RL

2 4 6 8 10 9 7 5 3 1
AD419 – 04/09

Copyright © 2009 Dorling Kindersley Limited, London
A Penguin Company

All rights reserved. No part of this publication may be reproduced, stored in a retrieval system, or transmitted in any form or by any means, electronic, mechanical, photocopying, recording, or otherwise, without the prior written permission of the copyright owner. A CIP catalogue record for this book is available from the British Library.

ISBN: 978-1-40533-665-9

Colour reproduction by MDP, UK
Printed and bound in Hong Kong

Discover more at
www.dk.com

Contents

Ancient Civilizations ... 4
THE MIDDLE EAST ... **6**
First Cities of Sumer ... 8
Babylon ... 10
The Assyrian Empire ... 12
Canaan ... 14
The Phoenicians ... 16
The Persian Empire ... 18
Riches of Arabia ... 20

AFRICA ... **22**
Egypt ... 24
Royal Tombs ... 26
African Kingdoms ... 28
Sub-Saharan Africa ... 30

EUROPE ... **32**
Monument Builders ... 34
Minoans and Mycenaeans ... 36
Classical Greece ... 38
Alexander's Empire ... 40
The Rise of Rome ... 42
The City of Rome ... 44
The Roman Empire ... 46
The Celtic Tribes ... 48

ASIA ... **50**
Indus Valley Civilization ... 52
Indian Empires ... 54
Steppe Nomads ... 56
The First Emperor of China ... 58
China's Golden Ages ... 60
Korea ... 62
Japan ... 64
Kingdoms of Southeast Asia ... 66

THE AMERICAS ... **68**
Early Mesoamerica ... 70
The Maya ... 72
Maya Beliefs ... 74
The Aztec Empire ... 76
Ancient South America ... 78
The Inca Empire ... 80
Mound Builders ... 82
Pueblo Farmers ... 84

AUSTRALASIA AND THE PACIFIC ... **86**
Australian Aborigines ... 88
Pacific Voyagers ... 90
Pacific Peoples ... 92
Glossary ... 94
Index ... 96

ANCIENT CIVILIZATIONS
Ancient Civilizations

A CIVILIZATION IS A HUMAN SOCIETY with complex organization. Throughout history, people have created many kinds of civilizations. These usually appeared once people stopped hunting and gathering wild foods and learned to farm. As a result of farming, more food was produced, so larger populations could be supported. Different classes developed, overseen by powerful rulers who were called kings. Most civilizations created organized religions, with gods worshipped in temples. Conflicts over land and religion led to many civilizations going to war with each other.

FLINT-BLADE set in a wooden handle

HUNTING AND GATHERING ▶

For much of human history, people lived by hunting wild animals and gathering wild plant foods – a way of life still followed in parts of the world, such as the African bush. Hunting and gathering can only support a small population, which often has to keep moving in pursuit of food. Although hunter-gatherers are sometimes called primitive, their way of life demands great skill and knowledge.

AFRICAN BUSHMAN PLAYS A MUSICAL BOW, CALLED A GORAH

SICKLE USED BY AN EARLY FARMER TO HARVEST WHEAT

▲ FARMING

Between 10000 and 8000 BCE, people living in some parts of the world learned to farm. Farming allowed people to settle in one place, at first in villages. These grew larger over time until the first towns emerged.

MUD-BRICKS were used to build the temple

PENS USED BY AN EGYPTIAN SCRIBE

▲ WRITING

Various writing systems were invented to keep records of business and government. The earliest are hieroglyphs in Egypt and cuneiform in Mesopotamia (Iraq). Writing was a widely respected skill, and experts, such as Egyptian scribes, had high status. Law codes, religious texts, poetry, and works of science and history were all written down.

KINGS ▶

Civilizations around the world developed kingship, with rulers displaying their importance in particular ways. The kings of many societies wore special crowns, donned lavish robes, and sat on thrones. The people they ruled over were expected to bow before them. In ancient civilizations, kings often claimed divine status. Egyptian pharaohs, for example, were worshipped as gods after they died.

EGYPTIAN PHARAOH WEARING A ROYAL HEADDRESS

BATTLE SCENE FROM AN ASSYRIAN CARVING, DATING 650 BCE

▲ WARFARE

The new way of life allowed societies to amass wealth, and led to competition over land and resources. From an early date, men went to war with each other. Many peoples went to war for religious reasons, fighting on behalf of their gods. Settled farming peoples were also raided by foreigners, such as nomads from the steppes of Asia. Warfare was a major cause of the collapse of many ancient civilizations.

▼ RELIGION

Farming peoples were at the mercy of nature and they worried about bad weather, which could destroy their crops. They worshipped gods linked with natural forces, such as the Sun and rain, and they asked these gods to protect them. In the early cities of Mesopotamia, they built great ziggurat temples where they worshipped their gods.

ZIGGURAT TEMPLE IN UR, BUILT IN ABOUT 2100 BCE

The Middle East

THE MIDDLE EAST, stretching from Anatolia (modern Turkey) in the west to Persia (modern Iran) in the east, was the birthplace of the world's earliest civilizations. In the Fertile Crescent, between Mesopotamia (modern Iraq) and Egypt, people first learned how to grow crops and domesticate animals. Farming villages grew into towns, which expanded into cities. It was here, also, that people developed the use of metals. They mixed copper and tin to make bronze, and later discovered how to use iron to make tools. The wealth of the cities brought merchants from across the Mediterranean and Arabia. It was in the Middle East that the earliest empires were created and some of the first recorded wars took place.

8–9 First Cities of Sumer

The very first cities, such as Ur and Uruk, were built by the people of Sumer in southern Mesopotamia. Sumer later became known as Babylonia.

Mosaic of a Sumerian army from Ur, dating from about 2500 BCE

10–11 Babylon

The magnificent city of Babylon stood beside the River Euphrates. For many years, the city was a centre of learning, famed for its astronomers.

Modern reconstruction of the Ishtar Gate, a ceremonial gateway in Babylon

12–13 The Assyrian Empire

To the north of Babylon, lay the land of the Assyrians, whose army was the most feared in the Middle East. Their empire flourished between the 10th and 7th centuries BCE.

Bronze doorway decorated with a relief of a war chariot

14–15 Canaan

Canaan, lying between Mesopotamia and Egypt, was subject to frequent invasions. One group who conquered coastal territory in Canaan was the Philistines in the 12th century BCE. Their neighbours to the east were the Israelites, who created the first religion based on a single God.

Egyptian carving of Philistine prisoners of war

16–17 The Phoenicians

Expert seafarers and navigators, the Phoenicians were another Canaanite people who grew wealthy through trade. Phoenician merchants founded settlements across the coasts of the Mediterranean, and exported cedar wood and purple dye. They sailed as far as Britain to trade for tin, and made the first recorded voyage around Africa.

Warship on a coin from Sidon, one of the most important Phoenician cities

18–19 The Persian Empire

Between 550 and 330 BCE, the Middle East, apart from Arabia, was conquered by the Persians, who created the largest empire the world had ever seen. The empire, which also stretched into Africa and Europe, reached its greatest size under King Darius I (ruled 522–486 BCE).

Stone relief showing Darius I, the Persian king, seated on his throne

20–21 Riches of Arabia

Wealthy trading kingdoms developed in Arabia, thanks to their control of the trade in incense. The incense was carried north to Mediterranean lands by camel caravans.

Frankincense (far left) and myrrh (left) were used to make incense

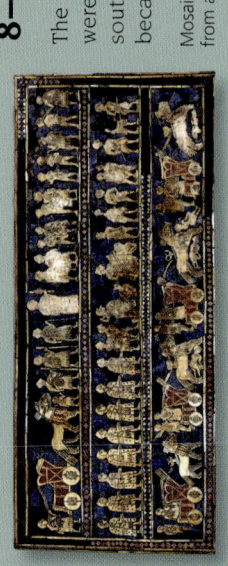

THE MIDDLE EAST
First Cities of Sumer

MESOPOTAMIA LIES BETWEEN the Tigris and the Euphrates rivers – an area that now covers much of modern Iraq. It was the ancient Greeks who named this region Mesopotamia, meaning "the land between the rivers". In about 5000 BCE, the farming people of Sumer founded small settlements that grew into the world's first cities, each with its own ruler and god. As Mesopotamia lacked raw materials, Sumerian merchants began to travel to distant lands, trading surplus food and luxury goods for stone, timber, and metals. By 3100 BCE, the Sumerians had developed cuneiform, one of the world's first known writing systems.

RIVER EUPHRATES

▲ THE RIVERS

Every year, the Tigris and the Euphrates rivers flooded. But this flooding took place too late in the year to water the crops, which were already growing in the fields. So the Sumerians worked together in organized groups, digging canals to irrigate the land and building reservoirs to store the floodwater for later use.

THE CITY OF UR ▶

The walled cities of Sumer contained a vast network of mud-brick houses, temples, and grand palaces. Each city was dominated by a huge temple tower called a ziggurat. The Sumerians worshipped many gods, and each city had its own patron god. The city of Ur was home to the Moon god Nanna.

THIS MAP SHOWS the major cities of Sumer (southern Mesopotamia), including Ur, Uruk, and Nippur.

TRADING SHIPS set sail from the harbour at Ur

MOSAIC ON A BOX

▲ KINGS AT WAR

Sumerian city-states were governed by kings, who claimed to rule on behalf of the local god. There were about a dozen city-states, whose kings often went to war with each other over land and resources. This mosaic from Ur shows a Sumerian king (middle top row) receiving prisoners captured in battle.

FIRST CITIES OF SUMER

CUNEIFORM TABLET FROM SUMER SHOWING RECORDS OF BARLEY RATIONS

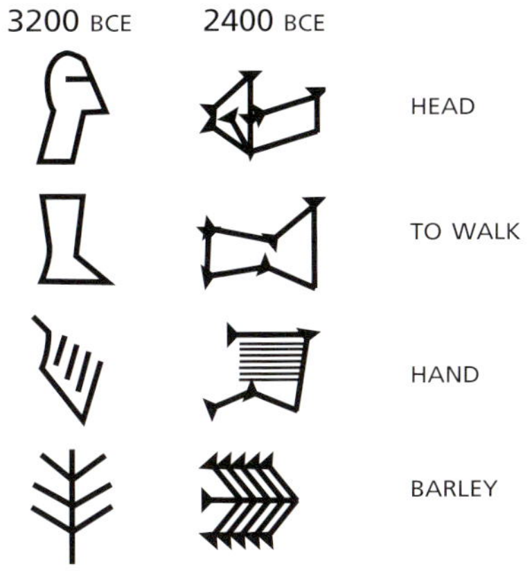

◄ WRITING

The need to keep records led to the invention of a writing system called cuneiform. At first, note-takers called scribes drew simple pictures on clay tablets. These pictograms developed into wedge-shaped symbols, made by pushing a cut reed into the clay. There were about 600 signs, which stood for sounds, words, and ideas.

◄ TRADE

The main Sumerian crop was barley, which was used to make bread and beer. To grind the barley into flour, the Sumerians used grindstones imported from the north. Other imported goods included timber for building, stone for sculpture, and copper and tin to make bronze. In return, the Sumerians exported barley, dates, pottery, woollen textiles, and bronze items.

DID YOU KNOW?

- The Sumerians were the first people to make wheeled vehicles. The idea probably developed from the potter's wheel, which was invented independently in Mesopotamia, Egypt, and China. Sumerian wheels were made from solid blocks of wood, without spokes.

3200 BCE	2400 BCE	
		HEAD
		TO WALK
		HAND
		BARLEY

CUNEIFORM SIGNS DEVELOPED FROM PICTOGRAMS (LEFT) TO STYLIZED SYMBOLS

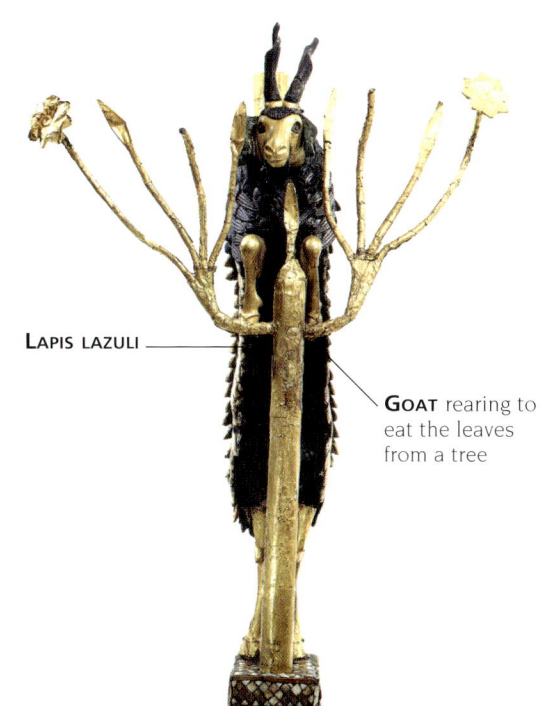

LAPIS LAZULI

GOAT rearing to eat the leaves from a tree

TREASURES OF UR ▲

In 1928, archaeologists discovered the tombs of the royal kings and queens at Ur. These tombs, filled with treasures, provided evidence of the skill of the Sumerian craftworkers, of the fabulous wealth of the royal courts, and of long distance trade. One artefact found was this statuette of a male goat, made of gold from Egypt and a blue stone called lapis lazuli from Afghanistan.

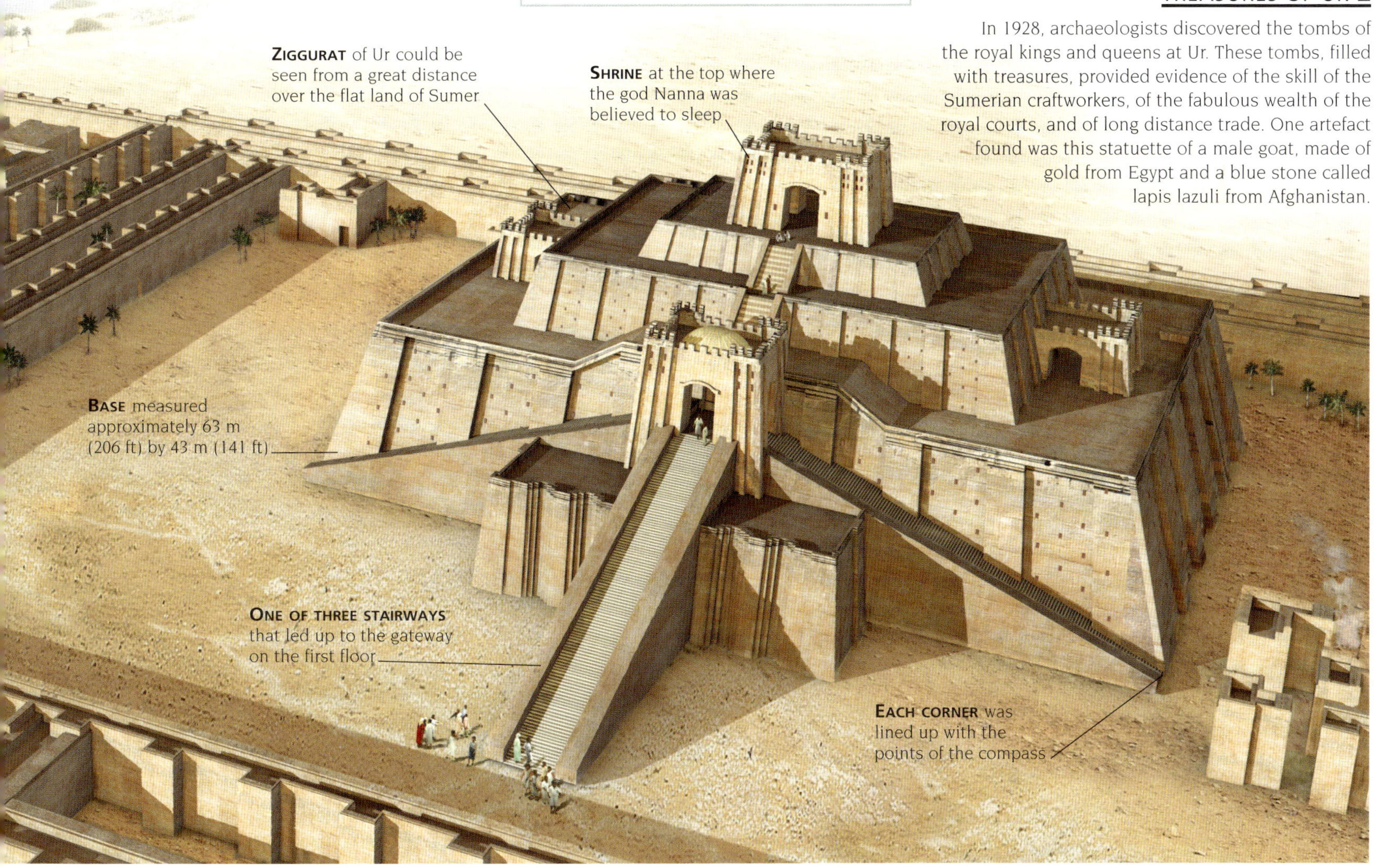

ZIGGURAT of Ur could be seen from a great distance over the flat land of Sumer

SHRINE at the top where the god Nanna was believed to sleep

BASE measured approximately 63 m (206 ft) by 43 m (141 ft)

ONE OF THREE STAIRWAYS that led up to the gateway on the first floor

EACH CORNER was lined up with the points of the compass

THE MIDDLE EAST

Babylon

THE MOST FAMOUS MESOPOTAMIAN CITY was Babylon, beside the River Euphrates. Twice in ancient history, the Babylonians ruled a large empire. Under King Hammurabi, Babylon ruled most of Mesopotamia (modern Iraq). The later empire of Nebuchadnezzar included much of the Near East. Babylon, which is thought to mean "Gate of the Gods", became an important centre of learning, and one of the most beautiful cities of the ancient world. Yet it is best known, from the Bible, as the place where, in the 6th century BCE, the Jews were exiled from their homeland.

THE MAP SHOWS the extent of the Babylonian Empire under Hammurabi (yellow) and under Nebuchadnezzar (yellow and green).

HAMMURABI'S LAWS ▶

In about 1792 BCE, Hammurabi inherited the Babylonian throne from his father. Babylon was just one of several city-states in Mesopotamia. In a series of wars against the other kingdoms, Hammurabi conquered them all. His most lasting achievement, however, was in establishing a set of 282 laws. These were carved on a stele (stone pillar), and set up in a public place for all to see.

PART OF THE STELE SHOWS HAMMURABI STANDING BEFORE SHAMASH, GOD OF JUSTICE

OUTER CIRCLE represents the ocean

BABYLON inside vertical band that represents the River Euphrates

◀ LEARNING

Babylon was a great centre of learning. This clay tablet, from about 600 BCE, is the oldest surviving map of the world, and shows Babylon in the centre, on the River Euphrates. The Babylonians also studied the heavens and created an accurate calendar, and they measured time in units of 60, the method we still use today.

BABYLON

▶ BABYLONIAN EXILE

After the end of Hammurabi's reign (1750 BCE), his empire broke up, and Babylon went into a long decline. The city only recovered during the reigns of King Nabopolassar (626–605 BCE) and his son, Nebuchadnezzar (605–562 BCE). A brilliant military leader, Nebuchadnezzar defeated Egypt, Tyre, and Judah. In 587 BCE, he destroyed Jerusalem, the holy capital of the Jews, and took the local people into captivity. The Jews spent fifty years in exile in Babylon.

NEBUCHADNEZZAR WITH CAPTIVE JEWS, FROM A 13TH-CENTURY GERMAN PRAYERBOOK

◀ THE ISHTAR GATE

Nebuchadnezzar embarked on a programme of building magnificent temples and palaces. In about 575 BCE, he built a gateway in Babylon, covered with blue tiles and images of dragons and bulls. Dedicated to Ishtar, the goddess of love, it was used as a starting point for religious processions. This modern copy of the Ishtar Gate has been built in Babylon.

DID YOU KNOW?

Babylon is famous for its Hanging Gardens, one of the Seven Wonders of the Ancient World. These gardens were supposedly built on raised terraces by Nebuchadnezzar, although no trace of them has ever been found.

Symbol of the Moon god Sin

Winged disk of the Sun god Shamash

Planet venus represents the goddess Ishtar

◀ THE LAST KING

Nabonidus was the last king of Babylon (ruled 556–539 BCE). He was especially devoted to Sin, the Moon god. This angered the priests of Marduk, the chief Babylonian god. In order to worship his favourite god, Nabonidus left Babylon, and lived in a desert oasis at Taima in Arabia. His reign ended when King Cyrus of Persia captured Babylon.

STELE SHOWS NABONIDUS WITH THE THREE SYMBOLS THAT REPRESENT GODS

THE MIDDLE EAST
The Assyrian Empire

THE ANCIENT KINGDOM OF ASSYRIA stood beside the River Tigris in northern Mesopotamia (modern-day Iraq). Between the 10th and 7th centuries BCE, the Assyrians were the most feared military power in the Near East. Their armies conquered an empire stretching from the Persian Gulf to the Mediterranean Sea. However, at the end of the 7th century BCE, their enemies joined forces to overthrow them. In 612 BCE, Nineveh, the last Assyrian capital, was sacked and destroyed.

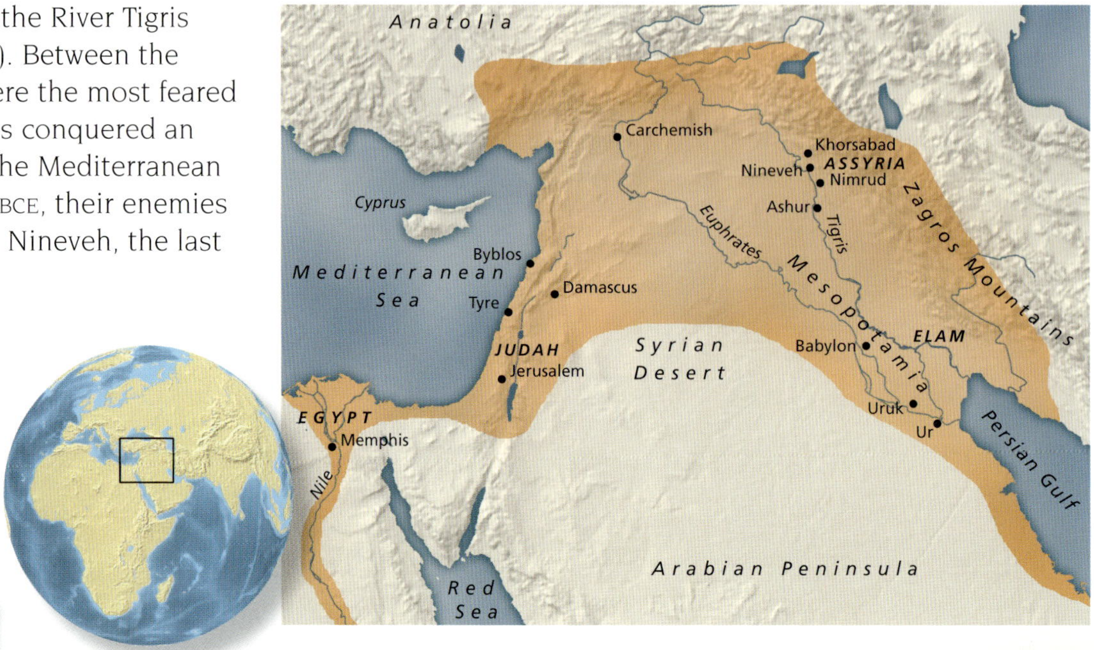

HORNED HEADDRESS, the Mesopotamian sign of a god

THE MAP ABOVE SHOWS the Assyrian Empire (orange) at its height in about 650 BCE, together with the royal capitals of Ashur, Nimrud, Khorsabad, and Nineveh.

CARVING OF A HUMAN-HEADED WINGED BULL FROM KHORSABAD

▲ PALACE LIFE

Assyrian kings claimed that they were chosen by the gods to rule over their subjects, who were mostly farmers. At different times, they ruled from capitals at Ashur, Nimrud, Khorsabad, and Nineveh. Here, they built huge palaces. Standing guard in the rooms were statues of human-headed winged lions and bulls, thought to protect the palace from demons.

ASSYRIAN ARCHER stands by in case the king needs help

KING ASHURBANIPAL stabs a lion through the chest

LION HUNT ▶

The kings showed off their skill and strength by hunting lions, which were captured and brought to royal hunting grounds in cages. The animals were released one at a time, and the king shot them with his bow. Here, the last great Assyrian king, Ashurbanipal (ruled 668 to about 627 BCE), is shown killing a lion.

THE ASSYRIAN EMPIRE

BRONZE DOOR PANEL FROM THE PALACE OF SHALMANESER III

◄ WAR

Assyrians prized warfare, and they decorated their palaces with scenes of their victories. Many scenes show battering rams and siege towers on wheels being used to capture fortified cities. This panel from a palace door shows a war chariot. Such chariots served as mobile firing platforms for archers. They were also used in mass charges, to smash into the enemy ranks.

STONE RELIEF FROM THE PALACE OF KING ASHURBANIPAL IN NINEVEH

CAPTIVES ►

Peoples who rebelled against Assyrian rule were severely punished. Thousands were taken away from their homelands and resettled in various parts of the Assyrian Empire, where they worked on building projects for Assyrian kings, while others were hung on poles as a warning to those who might still rebel. This relief shows the men, women, and children of Elam, to the east of Mesopotamia, being led into captivity in 646 BCE.

Layard and Botta

AUSTEN HENRY LAYARD   PAUL-ÉMILE BOTTA

The Assyrian palaces were rediscovered in the 1840s by Frenchman Paul-Émile Botta (1802–1870) and Austen Henry Layard (1817–1894), who was British. While Botta found the palace at Khorsabad, Layard discovered the palaces at Nineveh and Nimrud. They shipped many sculptures to France and Britain. As a result, the best places to see Assyrian sculpture today are museums in Paris and London.

RELIGION ►

The Assyrians worshipped a chief god, Ashur, whose high priest was the king. There were also many minor gods, called apkalle, who were thought to protect the king. These were shown in art with wings and the heads of eagles and lions. This eagle-headed god carries a pine cone, used to provide magical protection against evil.

CARVING OF AN EAGLE-HEADED GOD, DATING 8TH CENTURY BCE

LION HUNT RELIEF FROM THE PALACE OF NINEVEH

13

THE MIDDLE EAST
Canaan

During the late bronze age, from about 1550 to 1200 BCE, the region between Turkey and Egypt was known as Canaan. It was a land of city-states ruled by kings. In the 12th century BCE, waves of invaders, known as Sea Peoples, swept across the eastern Mediterranean. The Canaanite cities were sacked and one of the Sea Peoples, the Philistines, conquered the coastal strip. To meet the threat of the Philistines, twelve Canaanite hill tribes united in about 1020 BCE to form the kingdom of Israel.

The map shows the city-states of Canaan and the kingdom of Israel (red) at its height under King Solomon.

Carving showing hittite gods on the march

◀ THE HITTITES

From the 15th century BCE, most of Canaan was ruled by Egypt, and Canaanite kings were forced to pay tribute to the pharaoh. The Egyptians fought for control of Canaan with the Hittites, a war-like people from Anatolia (modern Turkey). In the 13th century BCE, the Hittite army conquered northern Canaan, but the Hittite Empire itself collapsed between 1200 and 1185 BCE.

CANAANITE KINGS ▼

The people of Canaan were farmers and merchants, who lived in small rival city-states such as Megiddo and Lachish. Each city was ruled by a king, who also controlled the surrounding villages and farmland. To protect their land, Canaanite kings built watchtowers and massive defensive walls made of stone.

Bronze statue of Baal dressed as an Egyptian

Ivory plaque showing musicians entertaining the king of Megiddo

◀ RELIGION

The Canaanites worshipped their gods at open-air shrines, usually on hilltops. These shrines were known as high places. Here, the priests sacrificed goats and other animals to gods such as Astarte, the goddess of love, and to Baal Hammon, the god of weather and crops.

THE PHILISTINES ▶

Between 1200 and 1150 BCE, the eastern Mediterranean was attacked by invaders known as the Sea Peoples. In 1180 BCE, the Sea Peoples were defeated by the Egyptians in a fierce naval battle off the coast of Egypt. After this defeat, one of the Sea Peoples, known as the Peleset or Philistines, settled on the coast of Canaan. This area was later named Palestine after them.

14TH-CENTURY MANUSCRIPT SHOWING THE FOUNDERS OF THE TWELVE TRIBES OF ISRAEL

WESTERN WALL, JERUSALEM

▲ THE KINGDOM OF ISRAEL

The hills of Canaan were home to the Hebrews, or Israelites. They were made up of twelve tribes and believed they were descended from a common ancestor, Jacob. Unlike most ancient peoples, they worshipped only one god, Yahweh. When, in the 11th century BCE, the Philistines seized their territory, the Hebrew tribes united to form the kingdom of Israel under the rule of their first king, Saul.

▲ JERUSALEM

David, the second Israelite king, was a great military leader. He drove back the invading Philistines and conquered the city of Jerusalem from the Jesubites, another Canaanite people. Here, David's son, King Solomon, built a great temple to their god. Nothing survives of the original temple, but the Western Wall of a later building is still a sacred site for Jews.

EGYPTIAN CARVING OF CAPTURED PHILISTINE WARRIORS

King Solomon

During the 10th century BCE, King Solomon ruled Israel for forty years. He was famous for his vast wealth and wisdom. He built his famous temple in the royal capital of Jerusalem to house the Ark of the Covenant, the box containing the tablets on which the Ten Commandments were written. After Solomon's death in about 922 BCE, Israel split into two kingdoms with Israel in the north and Judah in the south.

THE MIDDLE EAST
The Phoenicians

THE PHOENICIANS LIVED along the coast of modern-day Lebanon and Syria. They were a trading people who were the greatest seafarers of the ancient world. They sailed as far as Britain in search of tin, and made the first recorded voyage around Africa. Their search for wealth led them to set up colonies across the Mediterranean. The Phoenicians were not only traders but skilled craftworkers who specialised in ivory carving and metalwork. They also developed an alphabet system that formed the basis of all western writing systems.

THE MAP ABOVE shows Phoenicia (orange) and the areas colonized by the Phoenicians (yellow).

◀ TRADING CITIES
Phoenicia was made up of several independent city-states, the most important of which were Sidon, Tyre, and Byblos. In the 9th century BCE, merchants sailed from these cities and established colonies around the Mediterranean. In about 814 BCE, Phoenicians from Tyre founded the city of Carthage on the north coast of Africa. Carthage ruled a powerful empire between the 6th and 3rd centuries BCE.

COIN FROM THE CITY-STATE OF SIDON, SHOWING A PHOENICIAN SHIP

CEDAR FORESTS ▶
The hills of Phoenicia were covered with cedar forests, which supplied the Phoenicians with long, strong timbers, that were perfect for building. Both cedar oil and wood were exported to neighbouring lands, such as Egypt and Mesopotamia. In return, the Phoenicians bought raw materials, including ivory, copper, and tin.

CEDAR FORESTS, LEBANON

THE PHOENICIANS

Murex shell
houses the sea snail

▲ PURPLE DYE

The Phoenicians were famous for making purple dye, which they extracted from the mucus of the murex sea snail. Vast amounts of dye were made in the city of Tyre, where the snails were collected in large vats and left to rot, creating a very unpleasant smell. Phoenician purple cloth became highly sought after by other peoples, such as the Romans who used it to make ceremonial robes.

Phoenician alphabetic script

DID YOU KNOW?

▸ The name Phoenician is thought to come from a Greek word meaning "red". It may refer to the Phoenicians' purple dye or the reddish soil of their homeland. Another theory is that the name comes from an Egyptian word meaning "woodcutters".

◀ PHOENICIAN ALPHABET

By 1000 BCE, the Phoenicians had developed a simple alphabet, which formed the basis for all later western writing systems. Unlike Egyptian and Mesopotamian scripts, which had hundreds of signs, the Phoenician alphabet had just 22 letters, which stood for consonants. The alphabet, spread by Phoenician traders, was copied by the Greeks who later added sounds for vowels.

▼ SACRIFICE

Some people believe that the Phoenicians sacrificed their children as offerings to the gods. In Carthage, archaeologists discovered a sanctuary called a tophet, containing hundreds of carved stones, many of which were dedicated to the gods Tanit and Baal. They also found 6,000 urns holding the bones of very young children. No one knows if the children had been sacrificed or if they died naturally.

Carved headstones at the tophet of Carthage

The Persian Empire

IN THE 6TH CENTURY BCE Cyrus the Great (ruled 546–530 BCE) founded the Persian Empire. This vast realm spanned three continents, stretching from Egypt to northwest India. The Persian Empire was divided into twenty provinces, called satrapies, whose governors (satraps) ruled on behalf of the king. Persian kings received taxes and tribute from all over the empire, and rebellions were swiftly punished. Yet the Persians respected foreign customs, and each satrapy was allowed to keep its own laws, language, and religion.

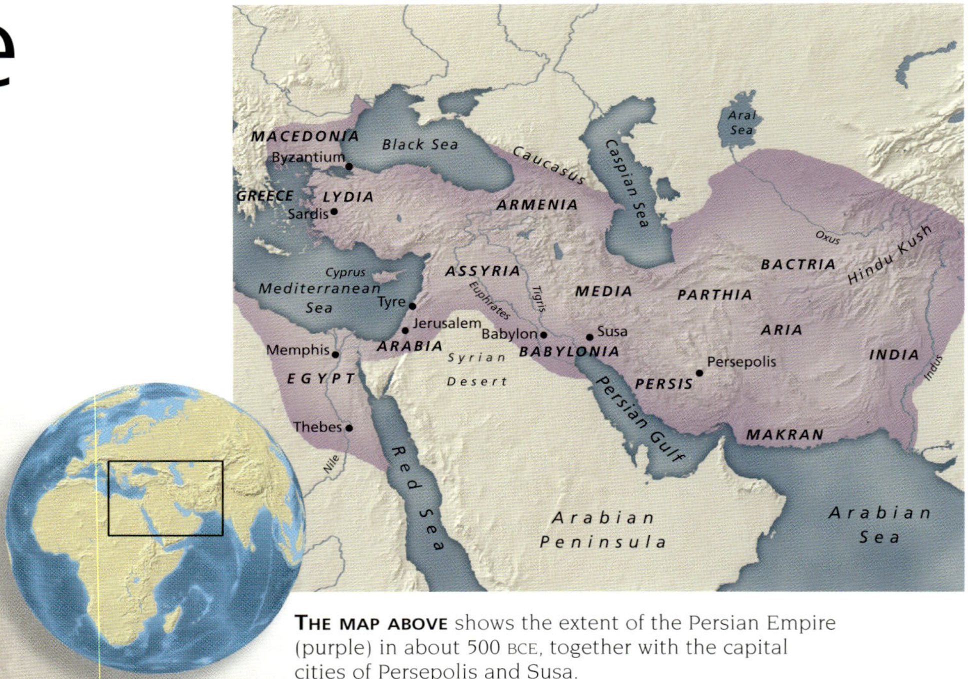

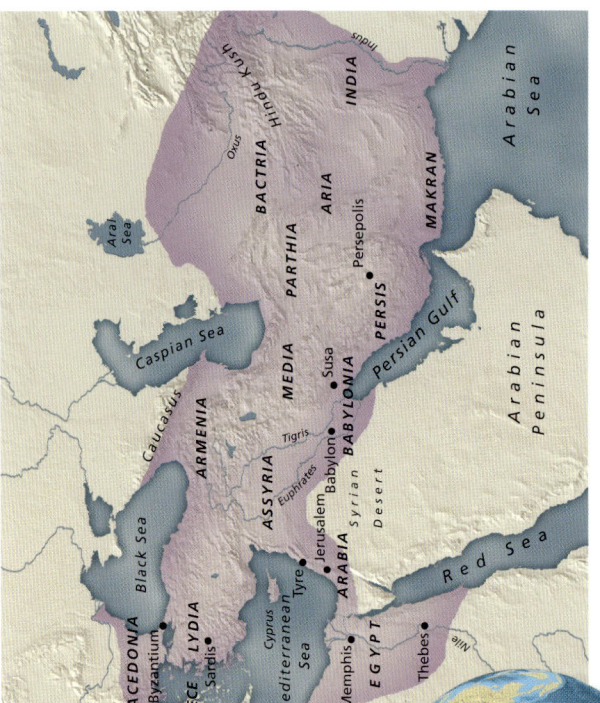

THE MAP ABOVE shows the extent of the Persian Empire (purple) in about 500 BCE, together with the capital cities of Persepolis and Susa.

◄ DARIUS THE GREAT

Under its fourth ruler, Darius I (522–486 BCE), the Persian Empire reached its greatest extent. Darius seized power following a civil war and put down several revolts across the empire. A talented military leader and gifted ruler, he organized the empire into satrapies and introduced a new coinage, the golden daric, named after himself.

DID YOU KNOW?

The Royal Road, built by Darius I, was 2,500 km (1,550 miles) long and linked Sardis in the west to the palace at Susa. At regular intervals, there were 111 post-stations with fresh horses for official messengers. Riding in relay, the messengers could cover the whole distance in a week.

GREEK VASE SHOWING A PERSIAN HORSEMAN FIGHTING GREEK FOOT SOLDIERS

THE PERSIAN WARS ►

In 490 BCE, Darius made a disastrous attempt to conquer Greece. Ten years later, his son, Xerxes (ruled 485–465 BCE) sent his army to Greece. The Greeks, led by the Spartans and Athenians, achieved yet another great victory over the Persians.

RELIEF SHOWING KING DARIUS I RECEIVING TRIBUTE

◄ AHURA MAZDA

Persian kings claimed that they were appointed by their supreme god, Ahura Mazda (meaning "Wise Lord"). He was thought to be the protector of the king and the Persian Empire, and was provided with an empty chariot drawn by white horses so that he could accompany Persian armies into battle. The god was represented in carvings as a man standing above a winged disk.

CARVING DEPICTS THE WINGED GOD AHURA MAZDA

THE PALACE OF PERSEPOLIS

Work on the palace of Persepolis started in 515 BCE, during the reign of Darius I. Xerxes later extended the palace. Persian kings used the magnificent halls to receive satraps and foreign ambassadors. With their vast size and towering columns, the halls were designed to impress visitors with the power of the Persian shahanshah ("king of kings").

① The 60-m- (197-ft-) square Apadana hall was built by Darius I.
② The columns were 20 m (65 ft) high and topped with carvings of bulls, lions, and eagles.
③ The walls were decorated with beautiful tiled reliefs.
④ The Hall of a Hundred Columns was built by Xerxes.

THE MIDDLE EAST
Riches of Arabia

ARABIA IS THE HOTTEST AND DRIEST part of the Middle East. Much of it is desert and semi-desert where Arabs lived in nomadic tribes. Some tribes settled in fertile areas near water holes, where they grew dates, barley, and millet. From about the 6th century BCE, five ancient kingdoms developed in the south and west. The southern states produced frankincense and myrrh, carried across the deserts by groups of camels called caravans. Towns on the trade routes flourished, such as Petra in the north of Arabia, while in the cities of Mecca and Medina, a new world religion, Islam, was born in the 7th century CE.

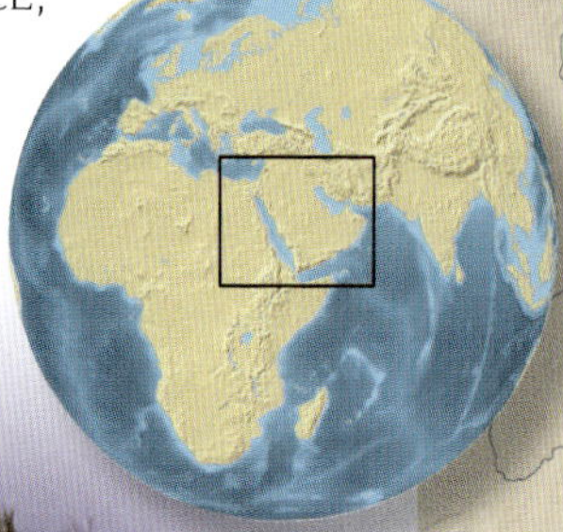

THE MAP ABOVE shows the major kingdoms of Arabia.

MODERN BEDOUIN TENT MADE FROM GOAT HAIR

▲ LIFE IN THE DESERT

On the edges of the desert, Arabs, called bedouin, lived as nomads, moving from place to place and sleeping in tents made from goat hair. With their camels, sheep, and goats, the bedouin travelled to towns and oases across Arabia, trading their wool and meat for dates, barley, saddles, and weapons.

INCENSE ▶

One of the most valuable trading products of southern Arabia was incense, made from the hardened resin of frankincense and myrrh trees. Myrrh, highly prized by the Egyptians, was used in embalming (preserving) the dead. Frankincense was made into perfume and burned in temple offerings to gods.

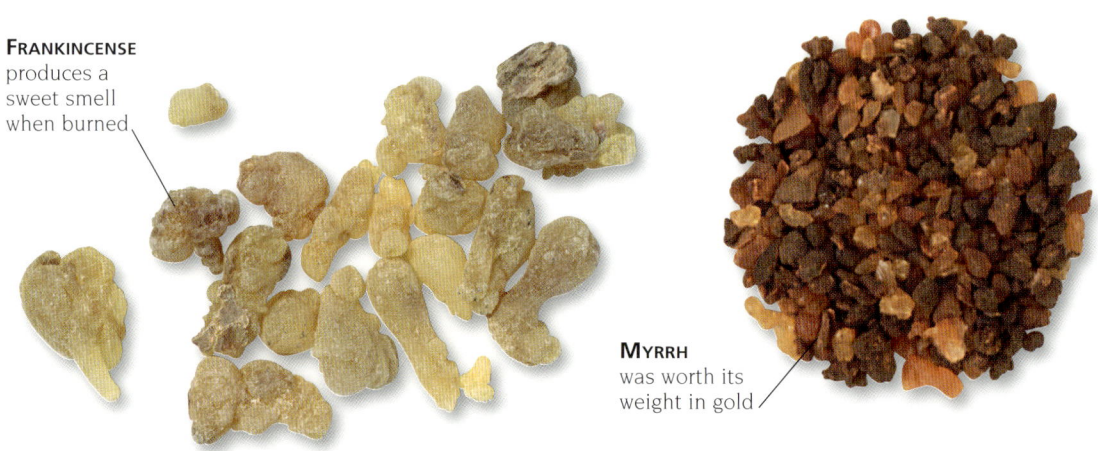

FRANKINCENSE produces a sweet smell when burned

MYRRH was worth its weight in gold

RICHES OF ARABIA

ROCK-CUT TOMB OF ED-DEIR, PETRA

◀ PETRA

At the northern end of the Arabian trade route was Nabataea. Its capital city, Petra, controlled the overland route for incense between southern Arabia and the Mediterranean. Petra would not have existed without trade, for the area has few local resources and is too dry for farming. Surrounded by cliffs, Petra is famous for its spectacular rock-cut tombs and monuments, with pillars modelled on Greek temples.

KAABA, THE HOLY SHRINE AT MECCA

▲ THE BIRTH OF ISLAM

The early Arabs worshipped many gods, including the Moon god and his wife, the Sun goddess. In the 7th century CE, Arab tribes were united by the Prophet Muhammad, who preached a new religion, Islam, based on the worship of a single God, Allah. After Muhammad's death, and spurred on by their faith, Arab armies conquered an empire stretching from Spain to India, creating a new civilization.

QUR'AN FROM THE 9TH CENTURY CE

▲ THE QUR'AN

Muslims believe that Muhammad regularly received messages from Allah through the Angel Gabriel. Muhammad's followers wrote down these messages in a sacred book called the Qur'an (meaning "recitation"). This edition of the Qur'an uses the earliest form of Arabic script, known as Kufic, which has straight lines and sharp angles.

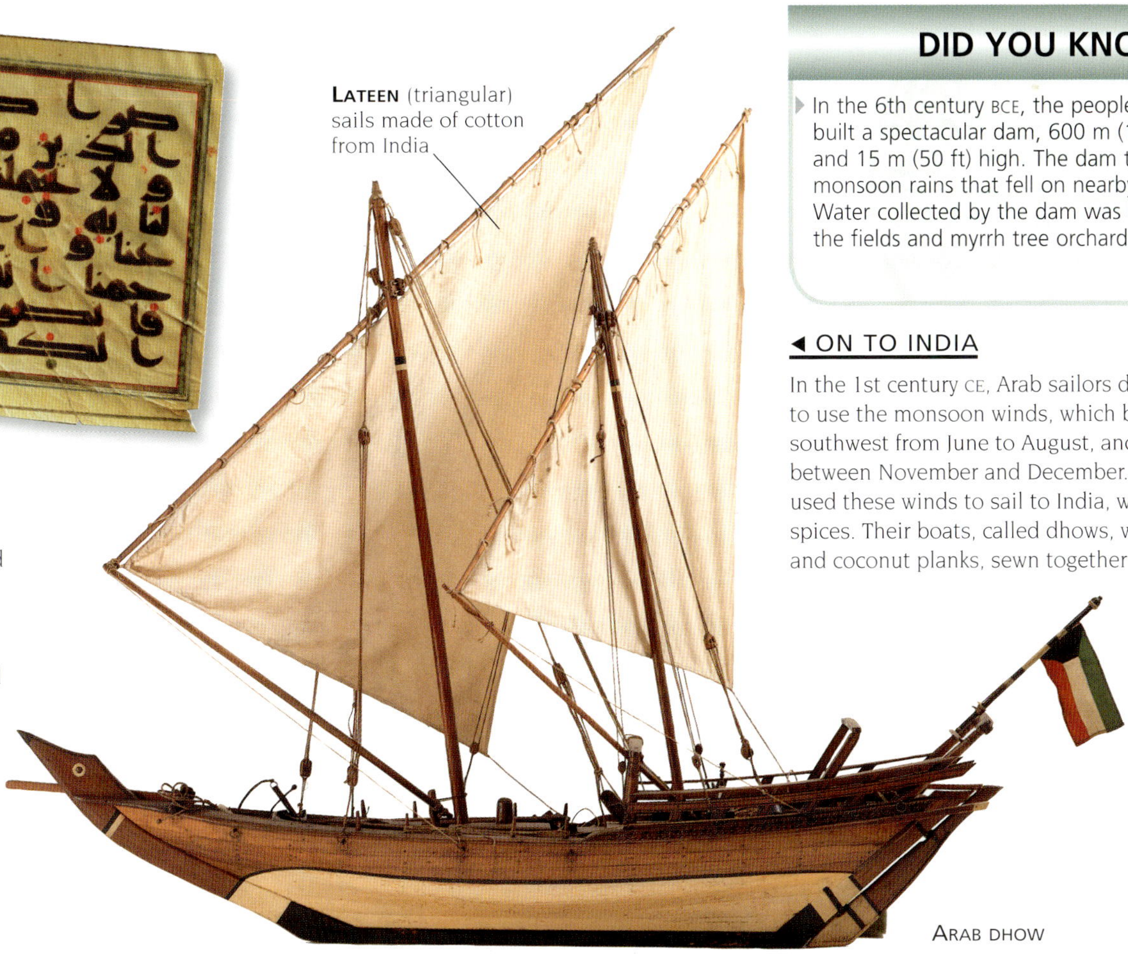

LATEEN (triangular) sails made of cotton from India

DID YOU KNOW?

▶ In the 6th century BCE, the people of Ma'rib built a spectacular dam, 600 m (1,970 ft) long and 15 m (50 ft) high. The dam trapped the monsoon rains that fell on nearby mountains. Water collected by the dam was used to irrigate the fields and myrrh tree orchards.

◀ ON TO INDIA

In the 1st century CE, Arab sailors discovered how to use the monsoon winds, which blow from the southwest from June to August, and from the northeast between November and December. Arab merchants used these winds to sail to India, where they traded for spices. Their boats, called dhows, were made of teak and coconut planks, sewn together with fibres.

ARAB DHOW

21

Africa

THE CONTINENT OF AFRICA includes vast deserts, thick jungle, and open grasslands. In the northeast, there is also the fertile River Nile valley, where the farming people of Egypt created one of the world's first civilizations. Later, the North African kingdoms of Meroë, Axum, and the Garamantes grew wealthy through farming and trade. South of the Sahara, people lived as hunter-gatherers until after 1000 BCE, when farming people, who also made iron tools, spread from their homeland in West Africa. Early evidence of sub-Saharan ironworking comes from the Nok people, who flourished in about 500 BCE. Later, from the 700s CE, the first states south of the Sahara appeared, in Ghana, Great Zimbabwe, and Benin.

24–25 Egypt

From around 3100 BCE, the Egyptians created the world's first state larger than a city. Its king, called the pharaoh, was thought to be a living god.

Model of an Egyptian farmer using a plough

26–27 Royal Tombs

Egyptian pharaohs built the world's first large stone buildings. Their pyramid tombs are still the largest stone buildings on Earth.

Pharaoh Djoser built the first pyramid, which had stepped sides

28–29 African Kingdoms

The North African kingdoms of Meroë, Axum, and the Garamantes were all home to farming and trading peoples. While the Garamantes traded with the Roman Empire, Meroë and Axum traded with Egypt, Arabia, and India.

Coin depicting King Joel of Axum

30–31 Sub-Saharan Africa

Powerful kingdoms also appeared south of the Sahara, in Ghana, Benin, and Great Zimbabwe. Like the North African kingdoms, the southern peoples drew their wealth from farming and trade, especially in gold, ivory, and slaves.

Edo people of Benin were skilled at making portrait heads in brass and bronze

AFRICA
Egypt

THE PEOPLE OF ANCIENT EGYPT created one of the world's earliest and longest-lasting civilizations. It began in about 6000 BCE, when farming villages spread along the banks of the River Nile. Eventually, two kingdoms were formed, Upper Egypt in the south and Lower Egypt in the north. In about 3100 BCE, the land was united when a king of Upper Egypt conquered the north. He was called the pharaoh, and was seen as a living god. The Egyptians built the first large stone buildings, including massive pyramid tombs for their pharaohs and temples for their many gods. They invented a writing system called hieroglyphs, and, as a river people, they made almost all their journeys by boat. Life in Egypt continued, with few changes, for almost 3,000 years.

THE MAP ABOVE shows Egypt, a long green strip beside the River Nile, protected from foreign invaders by the deserts to the east and west.

MODEL OF A NILE SAILING BOAT FROM A TOMB

▲ BOATS
Wooden sailing boats provided the main transport system, bringing stone from the quarries to building sites and food supplies from the fields to temples and towns. The prevailing wind in Egypt blows from the north, so sails were used to travel upriver. Travelling downriver, people rowed, carried along by the current.

▼ THE NILE
Egyptian civilization was only possible thanks to the River Nile, which flooded every year, leaving behind fertile black silt for farming. Hence, Egypt came to be called "the gift of the Nile". Beyond the narrow green strip of farmland, either side of the river, lay barren desert. Unlike the Mesopotamian rivers, the Nile flooded at the right time of year to plant crops. The farmers could grow two or even three crops in one season.

VILLAGES still line the banks of the River Nile

EGYPT

OXEN were used to pull the wooden plough

TOMB MODEL OF A FARMER PLOUGHING

▲ FARMING

Most Egyptians were peasants who worked in the fields as farmers. Their lives were governed by the Nile's cycle. While their fields were flooded, from July to October, they worked on building projects for the pharaoh. After the waters sank, in the autumn, they ploughed their fields and planted wheat and barley. In the spring, they harvested the crops.

◄ PHARAOHS

The pharaoh was Egypt's ruler and chief priest, and spent much of his time performing religious ceremonies. He was seen as the living representative of the sky god Horus, who took the form of a hawk. Thought to be divine, he was worshipped as a god after death. The word pharaoh comes from the Egyptian word "per-aa", meaning great house or palace.

STATUE is carved from an extremely hard stone called diorite

SCULPTURE SHOWING HORUS WITH HIS WINGS WRAPPED AROUND PHARAOH KHAFRE

◄ WRITING

The Egyptians invented one of the first writing systems, called hieroglyphs. These were picture signs standing for sounds, words, and ideas. Scribes, with their skill at writing, organized the harvest and the great building projects. By controlling the supply of materials, workers, and food, they made it possible to build pyramids and temples. Hieroglyphs were carved on stone or written on sheets of papyrus, a material made from water reeds.

CARVED OVAL was called a cartouche – royal names were written inside a cartouche

HIEROGLYPHS SHOWING THE ROYAL NAME OF PHARAOH RAMESES II

GODS AND GODDESSES ►

The Egyptians worshipped many gods, who watched over everything that happened on Earth and in the afterlife. Gods could take different forms, and might be shown as human or animal, or a mixture of the two. The Egyptians believed that the ram god Khnum was a potter, who made the first people out of clay, and also shaped every baby before it was born.

STATUE OF THE RAM GOD KHNUM

DID YOU KNOW?

▶ The River Nile, which was so important to the ancient Egyptians, flows from south to north. So when they learned about another large river, the Euphrates, the Egyptians were very surprised that it flowed the other way and named it the Upside-down River.

AFRICA
Royal Tombs

THE FIRST PERIOD of the ancient Egyptian civilization is known as the Old Kingdom (2649–2134 BCE). During this time, the Egyptians built huge tombs, called pyramids, for their pharaohs. The largest pyramid was the Great Pyramid of Giza, built by a pharaoh named Khufu. Later, during the New Kingdom (1550–1069 BCE), pharaohs were buried in secret underground tombs. Royal tombs were designed to last for eternity, and were made of stone rather than the mud-brick of the pharaohs' palaces.

DJOSER'S STEP PYRAMID

THOTH, the god of wisdom

▲ PYRAMIDS
Early pharaohs were buried beneath low mud-brick tombs called mastabas, which served as royal palaces in the afterlife. The first pyramid was created by a pharaoh named Djoser (ruled 2630–2611 BCE), who placed six stone mastabas of decreasing size on top of one another. Djoser's step pyramid may have represented a huge stairway, helping the dead pharaoh's spirit to climb into the sky. Some years later, a pharaoh called Sneferu (ruled 2575–2551 BCE) improved Djoser's design by building the first smooth-sided pyramids.

▲ LIFE AFTER DEATH
The Egyptians saw death as the beginning of a journey. Before they reached the afterlife, the dead had to travel through a dark underworld and pass a series of tests. In the New Kingdom, people were buried with papyrus scrolls containing prayers and hymns to help them on their journey to the next world. This papyrus scene shows a ceremony called the Weighing of the Heart, where the dead person is being judged by the gods.

COBRA represented Lower Egypt

VULTURE represented Upper Egypt

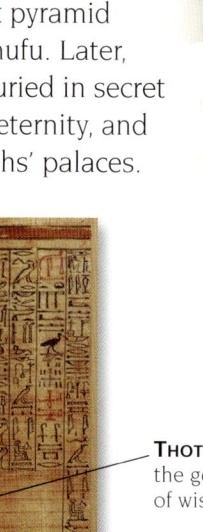

CANOPIC JARS

▲ MUMMIFICATION
Egyptians believed that, after death, the souls of the dead had to be reunited with their bodies, which were preserved in a process called mummification. The dead person's liver, stomach, intestines, and lungs were removed and stored in four containers called canopic jars, each protected by a different god. The body was then dried, stuffed, and wrapped with bandages.

◀ SECRET TOMBS
Pharaohs were buried with fabulous treasures. To prevent robbery, the kings of the New Kingdom built their tombs in secret locations to the west of their capital, Thebes. Despite this, almost all the tombs were robbed. The only tomb that has been found intact is that of Tutankhamun (ruled 1336–1327 BCE).

TUTANKHAMUN'S DEATH MASK

Khufu

This ivory statuette, just 7 cm (3 in) high, is the only known image of Khufu (ruled 2589–2566 BCE), the pharaoh who built the Great Pyramid of Giza. Khufu was the son of Sneferu, who built the first smooth-sided pyramids. Khufu was determined to outdo his father. Not only was his pyramid bigger than any other, it had the highest burial chamber and the deepest underground chamber.

THE GREAT PYRAMID OF GIZA

Khufu's tomb had the most complex interior layout of any pyramid, with three chambers and shafts pointing to the stars.

① Khufu's granite burial chamber.
② The middle chamber may have held a statue of Khufu.
③ The Grand Gallery led to Khufu's chamber.
④ The underground chamber was left unfinished.
⑤ One of two boats buried.
⑥ The tomb belonged to one of Khufu's wives.
⑦ Khufu's courtiers were buried in tombs called mastabas.
⑧ Temple where the dead Khufu was worshipped as a god.

AFRICA
African Kingdoms

To the west and south of Egypt, three other ancient kingdoms developed in North Africa. The first was in Nubia by the Nile. It had been governed by Egypt but, in the 11th century BCE, its people threw off Egyptian rule and set up their own kingdom called Kush (or Napata) and later Meroë. Rulers of Meroë modelled themselves on Egyptian pharaohs and built pyramid tombs. To the west of Egypt was the kingdom of the Garamantes. Its people were warriors who farmed in the desert using underground water. At the southern end of the Red Sea was Axum, a rich trading state in what is now Ethiopia, and one of the first states in the world to adopt Christianity as its official religion.

The map above shows the three ancient kingdoms of the Garamantes, Meroë, and Axum situated in the northern part of Africa.

KINGDOM OF THE GARAMANTES ▶

The kingdom of the Garamantes flourished from about 400 BCE to 600 CE. Named after their capital, Garama, the Garamantes were warriors who used four-horse chariots to raid neighbouring tribes to capture slaves. They traded with the Roman Empire, exchanging wheat, salt, slaves, and even wild animals for wine, olive oil, and pottery.

▼ FARMING IN THE DESERT

The Garamantes' greatest achievement was farming in the desert. They used slaves to dig tunnels under the sand, mining buried water. The water was then used for growing grapes, figs, sorghum (grain), pulses, barley, and wheat. Eventually, all the water ran out, and the civilization collapsed.

Rock carving of a Garamantian warrior on horseback

Ruins of Garama

AFRICAN KINGDOMS

GOLD PLAQUE SHOWING A KING OF MEROË WORSHIPPING THE EGYPTIAN GOD HORUS

RED SANDSTONE was used to build the pyramids

▲ KINGDOM OF MEROË

Meroë flourished between 400 BCE and 350 CE. The people of Meroë produced iron, which was traded as far as India. They were also the first Africans to grow and weave cotton, introduced from India.

▲ PYRAMIDS AT MEROË

The art, architecture, and religion of Meroë were all influenced by its neighbour, Egypt. The kings and nobles of Meroë even built pyramid tombs. These were very steep and ranged in height from 10 to 30 m (33 to 98 ft). The royal cemetery at Meroë was crowded with pyramids. In the 1820s, many of these pyramids had their tops smashed off by an Italian explorer, Giuseppe Ferlini, who was looking for treasure.

KING JOEL features on the front of the coin

COIN FROM THE REIGN OF KING JOEL (RULED 6TH CENTURY CE)

CHRISTIAN CROSS is shown on the back of the coin

▲ THE RICHES OF AXUM

After the fall of Meroë, Axum, a kingdom established in the 1st century CE, became the leading east African state, flourishing until the 10th century CE. Axum's wealth came from trading ivory and other goods across the Red Sea. Kings of Axum, who had converted to Christianity, issued coins with Christian crosses and royal portraits. Axumite coins have been found in Arabia, Egypt, and even as far as India.

DID YOU KNOW?

▶ Although we think of pyramids as Egyptian, twice as many were built in Nubia. While there are 90 Egyptian royal pyramids, Nubia has about 180. The Nubians were reviving a long-lost custom – the last Egyptian royal pyramid was finished in 1525 BCE, 800 years before the first Nubian one.

STELAE OF AXUM ▶

The best preserved Axumite remains are stelae, tall carved stones marking royal and noble graves. These were up to 30 m (98) ft high, and were carved to represent tall buildings with doors, windows, and the ends of wooden beams. This stela marks the grave of King Ezana (ruled about 321–360 CE), the first Axumite ruler to become a Christian.

AFRICA
Sub-Saharan Africa

From about 1000 BCE, Bantu-speaking peoples of Africa travelled south and east from their homeland in the grasslands of modern-day Nigeria. They moved into the tropical rainforests and the drier open savannah further south. The Bantu speakers were farming people and expert ironworkers. Over time, farming and ironworking spread across most of sub-Saharan Africa, together with the Bantu language. It was only in the very dry southwest regions that Africans, speaking other languages, continued to live as hunter-gatherers. Later, the first towns and states emerged, such as the trading kingdoms of Ghana and Benin in west Africa, and Great Zimbabwe in southeast Africa.

This map shows the areas where the Bantu speakers settled (green), together with some of the important cities and kingdoms that flourished in this region.

◀ IRONWORKING

Africans used iron to make weapons, axes, and hoes for farming. To do this, they heated iron-bearing rocks with burning charcoal in a tall clay furnace, a method still used today. Using bellows made from animal skin, they pumped air into the furnace through clay tubes. The result was a spongy mass, which was then heated and repeatedly beaten to remove impurities.

▼ FARMING

The staple African crops in the forests were tubers, such as yam and cassava. Another useful crop was the oil palm, whose fruits were boiled to extract oil used for cooking and for rubbing on the skin. In the drier savannah, farmers grew bulrush millet and sorghum (grain). Both plants tolerate drought, dying down in dry weather and growing again when the rains fall.

Modern clay furnace

Cassava

Yam

NOK CULTURE ▶

The earliest evidence of sub-Saharan African ironworking comes from the Nok culture, which flourished in what is now central Nigeria from about 500 BCE to 200 CE. Nok people lived in farming communities. They made iron tools for farming and produced pottery sculptures of human figures, often almost life-size. Many Nok figures resemble wooden sculptures, suggesting that there was also a woodcarving tradition.

Nok pottery sculpture of a human figure

SUB-SAHARAN AFRICA

GOLD OF GHANA ▶

One of the wealthiest states to develop south of the Sahara was the kingdom of Ghana in west Africa, which flourished from about the 8th to 13th centuries CE. Ghana's main source of wealth came from gold. From the 8th century CE, Arab merchants from the north coast of Africa crossed the Sahara on camels to trade for gold and ivory. In return, they brought salt, pottery, cowrie shells, and glass.

GOLD RING DECORATED WITH A LION FROM THE KINGDOM OF GHANA

BENIN ▶

From about the 11th century CE, the city of Benin in west Africa was the centre of a rich trading kingdom. Its ruler, known as the Oba, lived in a palace in the heart of the walled city. The people of Benin, the Edo, were warriors who raided neighbouring peoples to capture slaves. Benin itself was strongly defended with moats and ramparts made from earth. The last ruling Oba of Benin was deposed by the British in 1897.

BENIN BRONZE HEAD

DID YOU KNOW?

▶ Benin metalworkers were experts at making portrait heads in brass or bronze, using a method called lost wax casting. A clay sculpture was coated in beeswax and then covered in plaster. When hot metal was poured into the mould, it melted the wax, filling the space left behind.

GREAT ZIMBABWE ▼

One of the most important trading centres in southern Africa was the fortress city of Great Zimbabwe. Huge stone-walled enclosures, built between the 11th and 15th centuries CE, formed the centre of the city, whose wealth came from trade in iron, copper, salt, and ivory. The stone ruins at Great Zimbabwe, shown below, are the largest ancient structures in sub-Saharan Africa.

31

Europe

Farming had spread from the Middle East to northwest Europe by 4500 bce. People made huge stone monuments called megaliths. This Neolithic Age only ended with the arrival of bronze in about 2500 bce. The earliest European Bronze Age civilizations were the Minoans of Crete and the Mycenaeans of mainland Greece. During the later Classical Age (500–336 bce), the Greeks created one of the most influential European civilizations. King Alexander the Great of Macedon led a vast empire, spreading the Greek way of life into Asia. His achievement was matched by the Romans, who conquered the lands around the Mediterranean Sea.

34–35 Monument Builders

Many megaliths set up by Neolithic people served as tombs. Others, such as Stonehenge, were ceremonial sites, linked with the Sun's annual cycle.

Polished Neolithic stone axe

36–37 Minoans and Mycenaeans

The Minoans and Mycenaeans built palaces decorated with beautiful wall paintings. They were great traders, whose ships sailed the eastern Mediterranean. The Minoans also invented the first European writing system.

Gold death mask worn by a king of Mycenae

38–39 Classical Greece

During the Classical Age, the Greeks created great works of art, including paintings and sculptures. They lived in rival city-states, which were often at war with each other.

Greeks loved sports, such as long jump

40–41 Alexander's Empire

In the 4th century bce, the Greeks were united under King Alexander the Great of Macedon. Alexander conquered an empire stretching from Egypt to the borders of India, and the Greek way of life spread across the Middle East.

Roman mosaic showing Alexander riding into battle

42–43 The Rise of Rome

Between the 6th and 1st centuries bce, Rome grew from being a small city-state in Italy to the capital of an empire. In early times, the Romans were influenced by their Etruscan neighbours.

Etruscan bronze monster called a chimera

44–45 The City of Rome

By the 1st century ce, Rome was the largest city on Earth, with a population of more than 1,200,000 people. The city was filled with magnificent buildings.

Concrete dome of the Pantheon, a temple in Rome

46–47 The Roman Empire

Although the Roman Empire was well organized and long lasting, its western half was eventually conquered by Germanic invaders, such as the Vandals.

Mosaic detail of a Vandal lord

48–49 The Celtic Tribes

Before the Romans conquered most of western Europe, it was home to Celtic tribes. Only the Celts of Ireland and Scotland remained unconquered.

Celts made richly decorated bronze mirrors

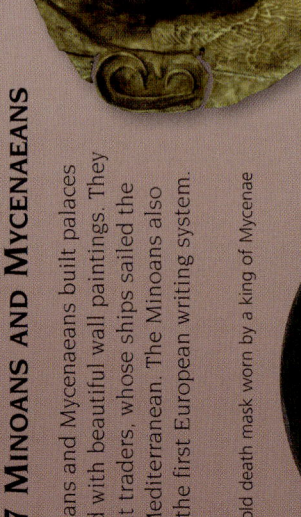

EUROPE
Monument Builders

By 4500 BCE, farming had spread from the Middle East to northwest Europe. This marked the beginning of the Neolithic (New Stone Age) period. Between 4000 and 2500 BCE, farming people across northwest Europe set up huge stone monuments called megaliths. Many were built as communal tombs. Others, such as circles and rows of standing stones, may have been used for religious ceremonies or to follow the movements of the Moon and Sun. The building of larger megaliths, such as Stonehenge in England and Carnac in France, show that Neolithic elites were able to mobilize vast numbers of people over long periods of time. They also show how ideas and customs spread along sea routes between western Europe, Britain, and Scandinavia.

THE MAP ABOVE shows the distribution of Neolithic megaliths (orange) in Europe.

◀ BURIAL CUSTOMS

Neolithic people built large and elaborate tombs to honour their dead. The biggest are passage graves, which had long stone-lined passages leading to inner burial chambers. This is the entrance to a huge passage grave at Newgrange in Ireland, whose outer wall is made of white quartz and dark granite. Above the doorway is an opening, designed to let the rising Sun shine into the burial chamber at midwinter.

▼ SKARA BRAE

Built in about 3000 BCE, Skara Brae is a wonderfully preserved Neolithic village in Orkney, off the coast of Scotland. The village consists of one-room houses containing stone furniture, such as seats, cupboards, and storage boxes. Orkney has few trees, so the roofs would have been made from driftwood or whalebone, covered with turf. The villagers grew crops, such as barley and wheat, and kept sheep, goats, and cattle.

PASSAGE GRAVE AT NEWGRANGE IN IRELAND, DATING FROM ABOUT 3200 BCE

SPIRAL PATTERNS decorate a stone in front of the entrance

RUINS OF A HOUSE AT SKARA BRAE

HEARTH where people burned seaweed or animal dung

SARSEN STONE could weigh as much as 50 tonnes (55 tons)

▲ STONEHENGE

The mysterious stone circle known as Stonehenge was built in southern Britain between 3100 and 2500 BCE. Stonehenge consisted of a double circle of blue sandstone blocks, which were transported from the Preseli mountains in Wales, 386 km (240 miles) away. Later, larger stones called sarsens, quarried locally, were added to the monument. These were set up as trilithons – an arrangement of two upright stones with a horizontal lintel stone on top.

◄ TOOL TRADE

From about 4000 BCE, Neolithic people began to grind and polish their stone axes to give them smooth surfaces. To do this, they used sand and water pastes and finely grained polishing stones. Polished axes were traded widely across Europe. Many were never used as tools, but kept as ornaments or status symbols.

POLISHED STONE AXE

CARNAC ▼

While people in Britain built circular stone monuments, the megaliths of northwest France were more commonly set up in rows, or avenues. At Carnac in France, more than 3,000 standing stones were placed in long parallel rows. The stones were set up over many generations, and it is thought that each megalith may have represented an ancestor, whose spirit lived on in the stone.

MEGALITHS OF CARNAC, FRANCE

STANDING STONES are about 6 m (20 ft) high

◄ FLINT MINING

Neolithic people discovered that flint lying in seams deep underground was better for making tools and weapons than surface flints. They mined for flint by digging through layers of soft chalk using picks made from deer antlers. The layer of flint in this Neolithic mine in England is 9 m (30 ft) below ground. Flint and chalk are both made from the skeletons of ancient sea creatures, which built up on the seabed 100–65 million years ago.

CHALK is a soft, white rock

FLINT LAYER made from seasponges and other creatures

DID YOU KNOW?

▸ The people who created Stonehenge also built a multi-ringed timber circle at Durrington Walls, just 3 km (2 miles) away. Animal bones found at the site indicate that huge feasts were held here. The timber circle may have represented the world of the living, while the stone circle probably stood for the dead ancestors.

EUROPE
Minoans and Mycenaeans

THE MAP ABOVE shows the sites of the Minoan palaces of Crete (black) and the fortress palaces of the Mycenaeans (pink) on mainland Greece.

By 2600 BCE, Europe's first advanced civilization developed on the island of Crete in the eastern Mediterranean. The Minoans of Crete built elaborate palaces decorated with beautiful wall paintings, and they invented their own writing system. They were great traders, who influenced the Mycenaean people of Greece. The Mycenaeans copied Minoan art, architecture, fashions, and writing. The Minoan civilization was at its height from 2000 BCE until about 1450 BCE, when all the palaces except Knossos were destroyed. The Mycenaeans, who may have destroyed the other palaces, took over Knossos, which they ruled until about 1100 BCE.

KNOSSOS ▶

The largest of the Minoan palaces was Knossos, which covered more than 13,000 square m (40,000 square ft). This vast, richly decorated palace was a seat of government, a religious centre, and an industrial complex, with workshops for potters, weavers and metalworkers. We do not know if Knossos was ruled by a king or by priests. When the Minoan civilization collapsed, Knossos was reoccupied by Mycenaeans.

WALL PAINTING OF A HARBOUR SCENE

▲ MINOAN TRADERS

The Minoans were expert sailors who grew wealthy from trade. Their merchants sailed all over the eastern Mediterranean, exchanging Cretan products, such as pottery, for foreign goods, including ivory from Egypt and copper from Cyprus. This painting from Thera (modern Santorini) shows a crowd welcoming a returning fleet. The people of Thera may have been Cretan settlers, or local people who copied Minoan fashions.

RECONSTRUCTED NORTH ENTRANCE OF THE PALACE AT KNOSSOS

MINOANS AND MYCENAEANS

LIONS stand guard over the gateway to Mycenae – the oldest monumental sculpture in Europe

▶ THE GODDESS
Minoans worshipped gods in special rooms in their palaces, and at outdoor shrines on mountain peaks and in caves. Here, they left offerings, including figurines of richly dressed women, accompanied by animals, such as lions and snakes. These suggest that goddesses were more important to the Minoans than male gods. The fact that this figurine, holding snakes, has a cat sitting on her head suggests that she is no ordinary woman, but a goddess.

SNAKES are sacred in many cultures and often linked with rebirth, since they shed their skin

POTTERY FIGURINE FROM KNOSSOS

▲ THE MYCENAEANS
The Mycenaean civilization of Greece, lasting from about 1600 to 1100 BCE, is named after the royal stronghold of Mycenae. There were several Mycenaean kingdoms, whose warrior kings ruled over a local population of farmers. Mycenaeans were much more war-like than the Minoans, and their citadels were defended by massive stone walls. Mycenaean kings ruled from palaces whose walls were decorated with scenes of hunting and warfare.

GOLD DEATH MASK OF A MYCENAEAN RULER FROM ABOUT 1550 BCE

▲ ROYAL GOLD
Early Mycenaean kings were buried in tombs, called shaft-graves, with vast amounts of gold, jewellery, and artefacts for the next life. When a king died, a death mask of beaten gold was placed over his face. This mask was found in 1876 by the German archaeologist Heinrich Schliemann. He was convinced it was the death mask of Agamemnon, a legendary king of Mycenae, but no one knows who it really belonged to.

GROUPS of straight lines represent numbers

MYCENAEAN LINEAR B SCRIPT WRITTEN ON A CLAY TABLET

▲ WRITING
The Minoans and Mycenaeans kept written records on clay tablets. The Minoans invented a writing system known as Linear A, which was made up of signs and pictures. The Mycenaeans adapted the Minoans' writing system and developed their own script known as Linear B. When experts deciphered Linear B in 1952, they discovered that it represented an early form of Greek.

Sir Arthur Evans
The palace at Knossos was discovered in 1900 by the British archaeologist Sir Arthur Evans (1851–1941). In the process, Evans discovered a previously unknown civilization. He named this civilization Minoan, after Minos, a legendary king of Crete.

EUROPE
Classical Greece

One of the world's most influential civilizations developed in Greece during a period known as the Classical Age (500–336 BCE). The ancient Greeks lived in rival city-states, sharing a common language, religion, and culture. A growing need for land from the late 9th century BCE, led the Greeks to spread out, founding colonies across the Mediterranean and the Black Sea. The Greeks made a huge contribution to western culture – in science, philosophy, politics, athletics, theatre, and the study of history. Yet they were also extremely competitive, and saw every activity, from sport to warfare, as a chance to win glory.

The map above shows the Greek homeland (orange), together with some of the leading city-states, such as Athens and Sparta. The overseas settlements and cities (yellow) were widely distributed.

▼ THE CITY-STATES

The Greeks lived in hundreds of separate city-states. Each city-state was called a polis, from which we get the word "politics". Although they shared the same language and culture, the city-states were independent, with their own laws, calendar, public assemblies, and coins. The leading city-states were Athens and Sparta. Bitter rivals, they fought a 27-year war against each other in the late 5th century BCE. Sparta was the final victor.

Parthenon in Athens, a temple to Athena, patron goddess of the city

Temple was made of marble, the most prized and expensive stone

Marble portrait of Pericles

▲ MEN OF POLITICS

Unlike other ancient states, which were ruled by kings, most Greek city-states were governed by assemblies of citizens. Usually, only the wealthiest citizens were allowed to take part. Athens, however, developed a system of government known as a democracy. Every adult male citizen could vote on important issues. One of Athen's most powerful politicians and generals was Pericles (c. 495–429 BCE).

DETAIL FROM A GREEK VASE SHOWING HOPLITES FIGHTING

▲ GREEKS AT WAR

When faced with a common threat, the city-states finally united in the 5th century BCE. An alliance of city-states, led by Sparta and Athens, fought off two Persian invasions. The main foot soldiers were the hoplites, who fought in a tight group called a phalanx, armed with jabbing spears.

GREEK COLONIES ▶

When the population of a city-state grew too large, its citizens often went to set up colonies elsewhere. In 690 BCE, Greeks from Rhodes and Crete sailed to Sicily in Italy, where they founded the colony of Gela. By 582 BCE, Gela had become overcrowded, and its people founded another colony further west at Akragas.

RUINS OF A GREEK TEMPLE AT AKRAGAS, SICILY

◀ SCIENCE AND PHILOSOPHY

The Greeks were pioneers in science and philosophy. Many sciences are still known by their Greek names, including physics, astronomy, and mathematics. Philosophers such as Plato (429–347 BCE) and Aristotle (384–322 BCE) studied human behaviour, and wrote about the ideal way to govern a state. Aristotle also invented logic, the science of reasoning.

GREEK PHILOSOPHERS IN ATHENS PAINTED IN 1511 BY THE ITALIAN ARTIST RAPHAEL

SPORT ▶

Every city-state had a gymnasium, where Greek men exercised and took part in sporting activities. The Greeks also invented sporting festivals such as the Olympic Games. This was a festival in honour of Zeus, the king of the gods, and people from all over the Greek world assembled to compete in these games. Events included running, wrestling, discus throwing, and the long jump.

DETAIL FROM A GREEK VASE SHOWING A LONG JUMPER

DID YOU KNOW?

▶ Theatre was invented by the Greeks some 2,500 years ago. Plays were originally put on as part of a festival in honour of Dionysus, the god of wine. Many modern words related to the theatre are Greek in origin, including actor, scene, mime, chorus, tragedy, and comedy.

EUROPE
Alexander's Empire

IN THE 4TH CENTURY BCE, the Greeks were united under the rule of Alexander the Great, the king of Macedon. Alexander was a talented military leader, who inspired great loyalty from his troops. After conquering Greece, Alexander invaded the Persian Empire in 334 BCE, before marching his troops into Egypt and finally on to India. By the time of his death at the age of 32, Alexander had conquered the largest empire in the world. During his long campaign, he founded new Greek-style cities across the empire, many of them named Alexandria after himself. The period after Alexander's death is known as the Hellenistic Age, when Greek language and culture spread throughout the empire.

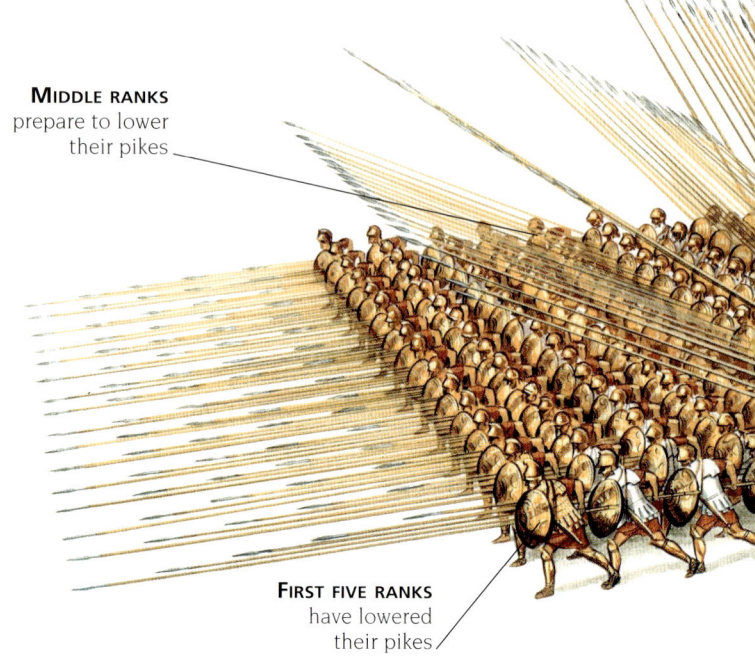

MIDDLE RANKS prepare to lower their pikes

FIRST FIVE RANKS have lowered their pikes

THE PHALANX ▲

Alexander's father, King Philip II, laid the basis for his son's military success, creating a powerful, professional Macedonian army. The foot soldiers fought in units of 256 men, arranged in a phalanx, 16 rows deep. They were armed with long pikes, called sarissas, which allowed them to spear their enemies from a safe distance. The Macedonian phalanx, which resembled a bristling hedgehog, could drive most enemies from the battlefield.

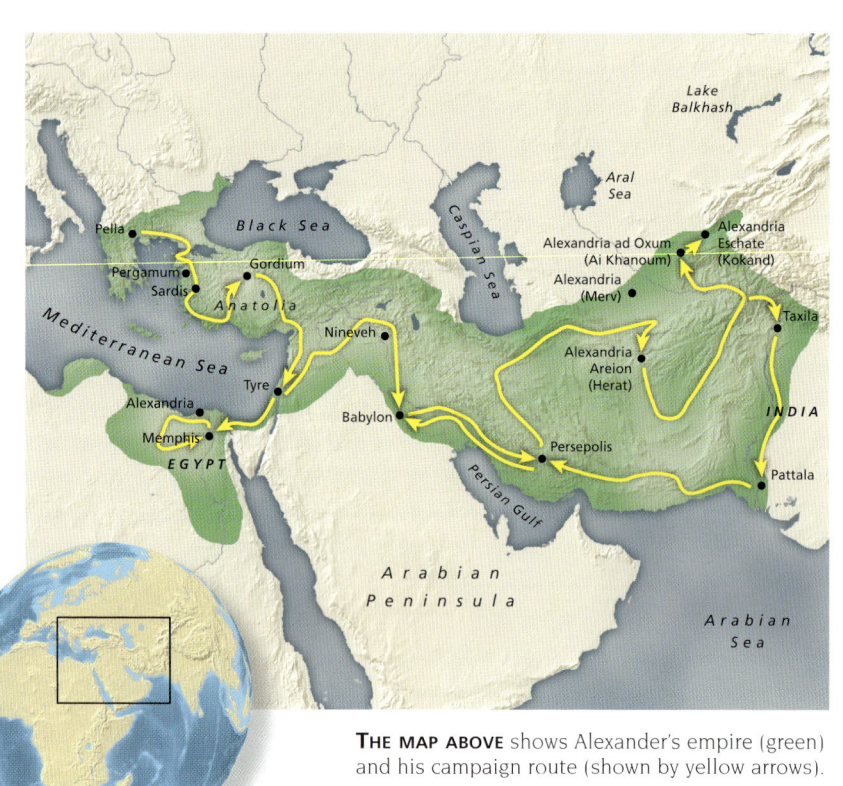

THE MAP ABOVE shows Alexander's empire (green) and his campaign route (shown by yellow arrows).

◀ KING PHILIP OF MACEDON

The Macedonian army was used by King Philip to dominate the Greek city-states. Planning to invade the Persian Empire, he forced the Greek cities to join him in a military alliance. However, in 336 BCE, Philip was murdered and his 20-year-old son took over as king.

SCULPTURE OF KING PHILIP

ALEXANDER THE GREAT ▶

Alexander won two great victories over the Persian king, Darius III, at Issus in 333 BCE and at Gaugamela in 331 BCE. On both occasions, Alexander charged straight for the Persian king, who fled from the battlefield. Alexander's armies went on to conquer the Persian city of Persepolis, leaving its palaces and temples in ruins.

ALEXANDER RIDING HIS FAVOURITE HORSE, BUCEPHALUS

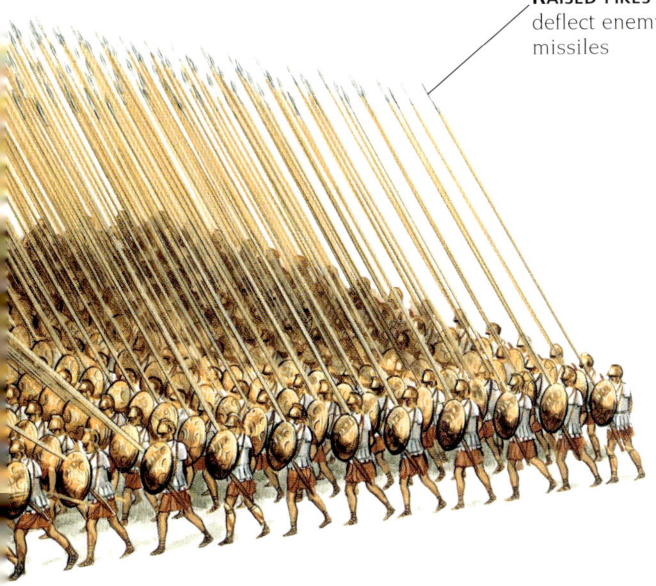

ALEXANDER'S EMPIRE

RAISED PIKES deflect enemy missiles

COIN SHOWING ALEXANDER'S VICTORY OVER KING PORUS

◀ **INTO INDIA**

In 326 BCE, Alexander invaded India, where he defeated an Indian king called Porus. He planned to conquer India, yet he had no knowledge of the country's vast size or climate. Alexander arrived during the wet season and the constant rain made conditions difficult for his exhausted army. Eventually, the troops refused to go on, and Alexander was forced to turn back.

Aristotle

From the age of 14, Alexander was taught by the great philosopher Aristotle (384–322 bce). He wrote on a wide range of subjects, including politics, medicine, and nature. In one book, *The History of Animals*, Aristotle described the structure and behaviour of more than 500 animal species. Alexander came to share his tutor's curiosity about the natural world, and his campaign in Asia was a journey of exploration as well as conquest.

ALEXANDRIA ▶

Alexander founded many new Greek-style cities. The most famous was Alexandria in Egypt, where his body was taken after his death. The city was the site of one of the Seven Wonders of the Ancient World – the Lighthouse of Alexandria.

LIGHTHOUSE OF ALEXANDRIA stood for more than 1,000 years

HELLENISM ▶

During the Hellenistic Age, people throughout western Asia began to adopt Greek customs and culture. They worshipped Greek gods, built Greek-style temples and public buildings, and went to the gymnasium and theatre. During this period, Greek became an international language, spoken by educated people across the Middle East. Shown here are the ruins of the Temple of Trajan in Pergamum, which was one of the Hellenistic cities of Asia.

EUROPE
The Rise of Rome

IN THE 6TH CENTURY BCE, Rome was a small city-state in Italy ruled by kings. By the end of the 1st century BCE, it had conquered the entire Mediterranean world. After the last king was driven out in 510 BCE, Rome became a republic. Led by an assembly called the Senate, Rome conquered the whole of Italy, and, between 246 and 146 BCE, went on to win three wars against the Carthaginian Empire of North Africa. In the same period, the Romans became involved in the eastern Mediterranean, where they took over the Greek states. In the 1st century BCE, after a series of civil wars, a general named Octavian (later known as Augustus) took over the republic and became Rome's first emperor.

THE MAP ABOVE shows the extent of the Roman Empire (purple) in the early 1st century CE.

◄ ETRUSCAN INFLUENCE

In early times, the Romans were dominated by the Etruscan people of northern Italy. The Etruscans lived in wealthy city-states, which were ruled by kings. Under their influence, Rome began to grow from a small village into a city. The Etruscans were skilled artists who created beautiful wall paintings and statues in terracotta and bronze. This bronze statue is of a mythical creature called a chimera.

◄ THE REPUBLIC

After the last king was driven out, Rome became a republic, governed by elected officials called magistrates. The most important magistrates were two consuls who were elected annually and acted as joint heads of state. They ruled with the advice of the Senate, an assembly of former magistrates, chosen from Rome's wealthiest and most powerful families. Shown here is a statue of a Roman lictor, an official who accompanied the consuls.

ROMAN CONQUESTS ►

After defeating Carthage for the final time in 146 BCE, the Romans destroyed the city. The same year saw the destruction of Corinth, which had led the Greek resistance to Rome. Both Corinth and Carthage were burned to the ground, and their people were sold into slavery. The Romans founded new cities on their ashes.

RUINS OF THE TEMPLE OF APOLLO, CORINTH

THE RISE OF ROME

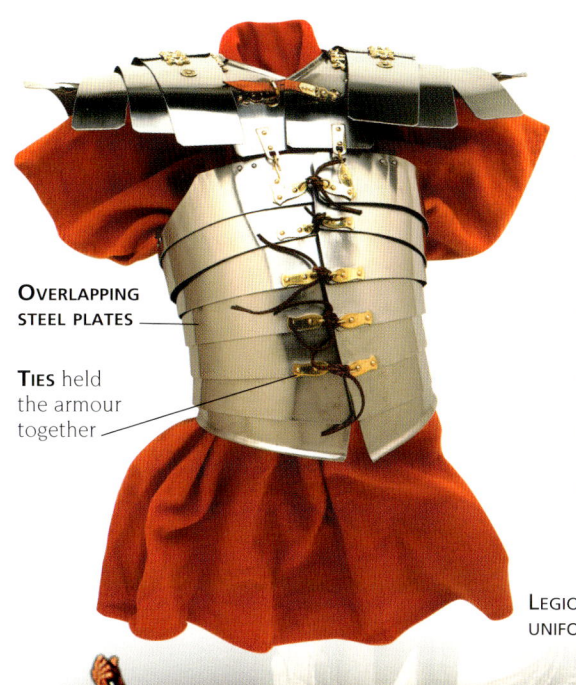

OVERLAPPING STEEL PLATES

TIES held the armour together

◀ THE ARMY

Rome's success was due to the discipline of its armies and its ability to win support from the peoples they conquered. The best soldiers in the Roman army were the legionaries. These were heavily armoured foot soldiers who carried long shields and were armed with javelins and short stabbing swords for close combat. Legionaries were Roman citizens who served as full-time professional soldiers. Fighting alongside them were non-citizen soldiers called auxiliaries.

LEGIONARY'S UNIFORM

RIGHT ARM raised in a gesture of command

LATE 18TH-CENTURY PAINTING SHOWING JULIUS CAESAR BEING ASSASSINATED

▲ CIVIL WARS

In the 1st century BCE, there was a series of bloody civil wars, in which ambitious Roman generals fought each other for power. The most successful was Julius Caesar, who made himself ruler of Rome. In 44 BCE, a group of leading senators stabbed Caesar to death, hoping to save the republic. His assassination only led to more civil wars.

THE FIRST EMPEROR ▶

The final victor of the civil wars was Octavian, Caesar's great nephew and heir. After defeating his enemies, he became Rome's first emperor, taking the name Augustus, meaning "the honoured one". Under Augustus, who ruled from 27 BCE to 14 CE, Rome became a monarchy. He made an outward show of consulting the Senate, but in reality, Augustus kept total control of the empire.

STATUE OF AUGUSTUS

Nero

The last member of Augustus's family to rule as emperor was Nero (ruled 54–68 CE). Ruthless and ambitious, Nero arranged the murders of both his mother and step-brother. He also shocked Rome's nobility by appearing on stage as an actor and singer. After Nero had dozens of leading Romans executed, there was a widespread rebellion against him. Abandoned by everyone, the emperor killed himself.

EUROPE

The City of Rome

IN THE 1ST CENTURY CE, Rome was the largest city on Earth with a population of at least 1,200,000 people, drawn from many different lands. It was a city full of magnificent public buildings, including temples, racetracks, theatres, bath-houses, and the Colosseum, where public shows were held. There were 11 aqueducts, supplying the city with water, and more than 40 parks and gardens. However, there were also slum districts, where the poor lived in badly constructed timber-framed apartment blocks, often with no running water or cooking facilities. With buildings crowded together, fire was a constant risk.

SENATE HOUSE still stands today

▲ THE FORUM

The centre of Rome's religious, ceremonial, and commercial life was a public space called the Forum, where people gathered to hear politicians speak and watch victory parades. Surrounding the central square were public buildings, such as temples, assembly halls, law courts known as basilicas, and the Curia, or Senate House, where senators met for regular meetings.

BATH-HOUSES ▶

Public bath-houses were busy social centres, where people could wash, relax, or take part in sport. Rome had five great bath-houses built by emperors wanting to gain popularity. One of the largest bath-houses, built by Emperor Caracalla (ruled 211–217 CE), could hold up to 1,500 people. Caracalla's baths included hot, warm, and cold rooms as well as shops, restaurants, and libraries.

RUINS OF THE BATHS OF CARACALLA

◀ CIRCUS MAXIMUS

The most popular and exciting spectator sport in Rome was chariot racing, which took place at a track called a circus. The largest track was the Circus Maximus, which could hold an audience of up to 255,000 people. The charioteers belonged to four rival teams, each with its own set of devoted fans.

SPINA – a central spine running down the course

METAE – turning posts of gilded bronze

QUADRIGA – a four-horse chariot

DID YOU KNOW?

Rome had the first professional fire service. The firemen were called vigiles (watchmen). Across the city, there were seven barracks, each home to a unit of 1,000 vigiles.

◀ THE PANTHEON

One of the best-preserved temples in Rome is the Pantheon. Completed in about 128 CE, its most spectacular feature is its concrete dome, which has 140 rectangular recessed squares that were designed to reduce the ceiling's weight. The Romans were the first to build using domes.

THE COLOSSEUM

The Colosseum was built between 72 and 80 CE by Emperor Vespasian and his son, Titus. Beneath the Colosseum there was a network of tunnels and cells, where wild animals were kept. Criminals were also held here awaiting execution.

① The gladiators, usually slaves, fought in pairs.

② Animals were let into the arena through the hidden trapdoors.

③ The senators sat at the front of the Colosseum.

④ Women and slaves stood at the back.

⑤ Huge linen awning, called the velarium.

EUROPE
The Roman Empire

THE ROMANS CREATED one of the biggest and best-organized empires in history. Across their state, they built towns and roads, spreading their way of life. By the 2nd century CE, people in far-flung lands dressed in Roman clothes, used the same Roman coins, and worshipped Roman gods. People were united by language, speaking Latin in the west and Greek in the east. Merchants could travel easily from one place to another, since all the lands around the Mediterranean belonged to the same single state. The empire's wealth drew traders from distant lands, bringing spices from India and silk from China. Yet it was the wealth of the empire that would eventually attract foreign invaders and lead to its downfall.

THIS MAP SHOWS the Roman Empire (purple) during the reign of Emperor Hadrian.

GROWTH OF THE EMPIRE ▶

Until 117 CE, the Roman Empire continued to expand. It reached its greatest size under Emperor Trajan (ruled 98–117 CE) who conquered Dacia (modern Romania) and Mesopotamia (modern Iraq). However, his successor, Hadrian (ruled 117–138 CE), believed that the empire had become too vast to control and gave up many of Trajan's conquests. Hadrian strengthened the empire with frontier defences, including a wall that ran for 117 km (73 miles) across northern Britain.

▼ ROADS

Roman soldiers constructed a vast network of straight roads that enabled their armies and official messengers to move rapidly throughout the empire. The roads had deep foundations and curved surfaces so that rain water drained into ditches along the sides. The network of roads also helped civilians, such as farmers and traders, to transport goods from one town to another.

HADRIAN'S WALL, BRITAIN

RUINS OF A ROMAN ROAD IN ITALY

THE ROMAN EMPIRE

PONT DU GARD, A STONE AQUEDUCT IN SOUTHERN FRANCE

MOSAIC SHOWING SLAVES TREADING GRAPES TO MAKE WINE

▲ BUILDINGS

The Romans were highly skilled builders and engineers. They pioneered the use of brick and invented concrete, a new material that was strong and relatively easy to use. The Romans also began to use arches to build bridges, aqueducts, and viaducts across wide valleys and rivers. The aqueducts, which carried water to towns and cities, tilted slightly downwards to ensure a steady flow of water.

SACRIFICED BULL – its blood was thought to give life to the Universe

LONG HAIR shows the Vandal's Germanic origins

MARBLE STATUE OF MITHRAS KILLING A SACRED BULL

▲ FARMING WITH SLAVES

The Roman Empire depended on slave labour. In many areas, slaves worked on huge farming estates owned by wealthy Romans. These estates were run by a vilicus (steward) who was usually a slave himself. The main crops produced on the estates were wheat, olives, and grapes for making wine.

◀ NEW GODS

The Romans worshipped hundreds of different gods who were responsible for different areas of life. The chief god was Jupiter, the sky god and special protector of the Roman Empire. The Romans also worshipped household gods who were thought to protect their homes and families. As the empire expanded, the Romans began to adopt new gods into their religion such as Mithras, a Persian god.

Constantine

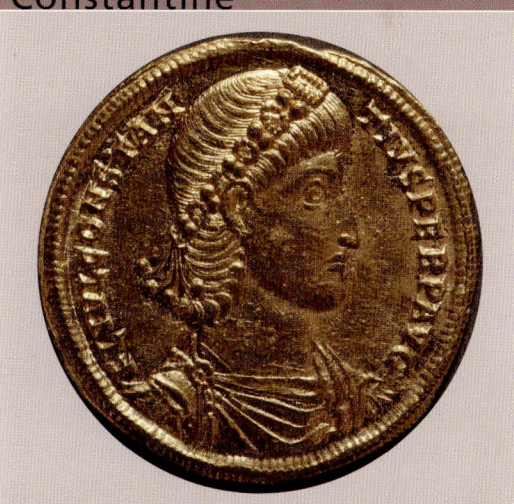

The empire was given a new direction by Constantine who was proclaimed emperor in the west in 306 CE, and was ruler of the whole empire between 324 and 337 CE. Constantine was a follower of Christianity, a religion that earlier emperors had tried to suppress. He founded a new Christian capital in the east called Constantinople. Christianity eventually became the state religion.

MOSAIC OF A VANDAL LORD HUNTING ON HORSEBACK

▲ FALL OF THE WEST

In the 5th century CE, the empire in the west was overwhelmed by Germanic invaders, including the Vandals. The Vandals did not want to destroy the empire but to share in its wealth. In north Africa, Vandal lords adopted the Roman lifestyle, living in houses decorated with mosaics. Although the west fell, the eastern empire survived for a thousand years.

47

EUROPE
The Celtic Tribes

Before the romans conquered most of western Europe, it was home to the Celts. They lived in many tribes, and did not think of themselves as a single people. Yet they spoke similar Celtic languages, related to modern Welsh, and shared similar customs, religious beliefs, and styles of art. The Celts were a farming people ruled by warriors. Often at war with each other, they built strongly defended settlements. They were skilled metalworkers and used iron to make tools and weapons, and bronze for decorated mirrors and shields. The Celtic civilization was at its height between the 6th and 1st centuries BCE.

The map shows the western European homeland of the Celts, with their Germanic neighbours to the east.

SOCIETY ▶

The Celts lived in large tribes ruled by chieftains or kings and queens. There were different classes, with a rich landowning warrior aristocracy at the top. There were also bards (poets), merchants, artists, skilled craftsmen, and priests called druids. Most people were farmers, who used a variety of iron tools. They cleared the land for farming using iron axes, and turned the soil with iron-tipped ploughs.

Plough tip

Iron tools of a celtic farmer

▼ HILL FORTS

In Britain, tribes built strongly defended hill forts, which resembled small towns. Maiden Castle in southern England had elaborate defences, with a maze of ditches to confuse attackers, and earth banks topped with timber ramparts. Maiden Castle would have been home to several hundred people living in thatched timber roundhouses.

Maiden castle, stronghold of the durotriges tribe

THE CELTIC TRIBES

◀ RELIGIOUS BELIEFS

The Celts believed in many gods and goddesses. The druids sacrificed objects and sometimes people to their gods. Celts also practised head-hunting, believing that the head contained a person's soul and life-force. Taking an enemy's head in battle was a way of capturing his power.

SKULLS were probably those of enemies, killed in war

PATTERN may have been laid out using a metal compass

NICHE for another skull, now missing

MIRROR FROM DESBOROUGH IN BRITAIN

▲ CELTIC ART

Celtic artists loved making rich patterns with spirals and swirls, which they used to decorate bronze artefacts, such as shields and the backs of mirrors. In Ireland and Scotland, which were never conquered by the Romans, Celtic art survived into the Middle Ages. Celtic patterns, like those on this mirror, are found in medieval Irish Bibles.

CELTIC SANCTUARY IN ROQUEPERTUSE, FRANCE

Vercingetorix

A noble from the Averni tribe, Vercingetorix (82–46 BCE) was a Celtic war leader from Gaul (France). In 52 BCE, he led an uprising against the Roman general Julius Caesar, who had recently conquered Gaul. Through force of personality, Vercingetorix united several tribes. Despite early successes, he was defeated and captured. After being paraded in Caesar's triumphal procession in Rome, Vercingetorix was executed.

▼ WARRIORS

Although fierce and brave in battle, Celts fought as individual warriors, each hoping to win personal glory. In battle, they were usually defeated by the Romans, who fought in tightly disciplined groups. As a result, by the 1st century CE, the Romans had conquered most of the Celtic tribes.

METAL RELIEF FOUND AT GUNDESTRUP IN DENMARK SHOWING CELTIC WARRIORS ON HORSEBACK AND ON FOOT

Asia

THE LARGEST CONTINUOUS LANDMASS, Asia includes two of the world's oldest and most influential civilizations, China and India. China, unified by the First Emperor, was the most stable and lasting Asian state, and reached a golden age during the Han and Tang dynasties. Under Chinese influence, other early kingdoms formed in Korea and Japan. India, united by the Mauryan and the Gupta Empires, was the birthplace of the Hindu and Buddhist religions, which spread across Asia. Southeast Asian kingdoms, such as Champa in Vietnam, adopted Hinduism and Buddhism, and built Indian-style temples.

52–53 The Indus Valley Civilization

One of the world's earliest civilizations developed beside the River Indus in northwest India. The Indus people, whose civilization lasted from about 2500 to 1800 BCE, built the world's first planned cities.

Indus seal decorated with a bull and writing (not deciphered)

54–55 Indian Empires

Between about 321 and 185 BCE, India was united for the first time under the rule of the Mauryans. Later, a second smaller Indian empire was founded by the Guptas (320–554 CE).

Statuette of the Hindu god Shiva

56–57 Steppe Nomads

The vast, grassy plains of Asia are called steppes. These were once home to nomadic tribes who moved from place to place with their animals, looking for fresh pasture.

Metal ornament showing a stag from a nomad's tomb

58–59 The First Emperor of China

In 221 BCE, China was united by the First Emperor, Shi Huangdi, who used force to impose the same way of life across the country in order to preserve the newly united state.

Portrait of Shi Huangdi

60–61 China's Golden Ages

Chinese civilization reached a peak under the Han (206 BCE–220 CE) and Tang (618–907 CE) dynasties, which provided long periods of stable government.

Printed book – one of many Chinese inventions

62–63 Korea

From 57 BCE until 668 CE, Korea was divided into three kingdoms – Baekje, Silla, and Koguryo, all influenced by China. The country was then united by the kings of Silla, who had converted to Buddhism after it was introduced from China.

Bulguksa Buddhist temple from Silla

64–65 Japan

Between the 4th and 6th centuries CE, Japan was united by the Yamato emperors, who imitated the Chinese system of government.

Tomb of Emperor Nintoku, built in about 500 CE

66–67 Kingdoms of Southeast Asia

From the 8th to the 15th centuries, southeast Asia was a land of powerful kingdoms. The kings built great temples in honour of the Buddha and Hindu gods.

Temple tower, built by the Champa kingdom of Vietnam

MAP KEY

- Indus Civilization
- Mauryan Empire
- Gupta Empire
- Scythians
- Tang Empire (Later Period)
- Han Empire
- Khmer Empire
- Koguryo Kingdom
- Baekje Kingdom
- Silla Kingdom
- Srivijaya Empire
- Champa Kingdom
- Dai Viet Kingdom
- Pagan Kingdom

ASIA
Indus Valley Civilization

THE PLAIN OF THE RIVER INDUS, in northwest India, saw the development of one of the first great early civilizations. From about 2600 BCE, the people of the Indus Valley began to build the world's first planned cities – the most important of which was Mohenjo-Daro. At its height, the city had a population of up to 40,000 people and contained large public buildings made of mud-bricks. Indus people were expert builders, who developed sophisticated water and drainage systems. They manufactured goods, such as cotton textiles, and traded with their neighbours using a network of rivers. Little is known about how the Indus Valley cities were governed. No evidence has been found of temples, kings, royal tombs, or warfare, and, although Indus people developed a system of writing, their script remains undeciphered.

THE MAP ABOVE shows the extent of the Indus civilization (brown).

MOHENJO-DARO ▼
Mohenjo-Daro is the best preserved Indus city. It was built on a grid pattern, with the main streets exactly twice the width of the side streets. Like most Indus cities, it was divided into two areas. The lower city contained craft workshops and houses, built around central courtyards. On the higher ground was a walled area, housing important public buildings such as assembly halls, the granary, and the bath-house.

RUINS OF MOHENJO-DARO

GREAT BATH may have been used for ritual bathing

INDUS DRAIN

▲ WATER CONTROL
Indus builders were highly skilled in water management. Every house had its own water supply, toilet, and bath, with drains to carry away the dirty water. Beneath the streets, there were deep brick-lined sewers, with manholes to allow regular cleaning. Baths were waterproofed with a tarry substance called bitumen.

INDUS VALLEY CIVILIZATION

SEAL SHOWING INDUS SCRIPT ABOVE A PICTURE OF A BULL

▲ INDUS SCRIPT
Indus people created a writing system that contained up to 400 picture signs. The script, which has not been deciphered, was carved on stone seals, together with pictures of animals, humans, and mythical figures. Each seal may show the name and emblem of a particular family.

INDUS CLOTHES ▶
The Indus people were among the first in the world to make cloth from the fibrous seed coats of the cotton plant. The cotton was then woven into robes and short skirts. Pottery figures found in the Indus Valley give an indication of the kinds of clothes worn by its inhabitants. This female figure wears a belt, two necklaces, and a fan-shaped headdress.

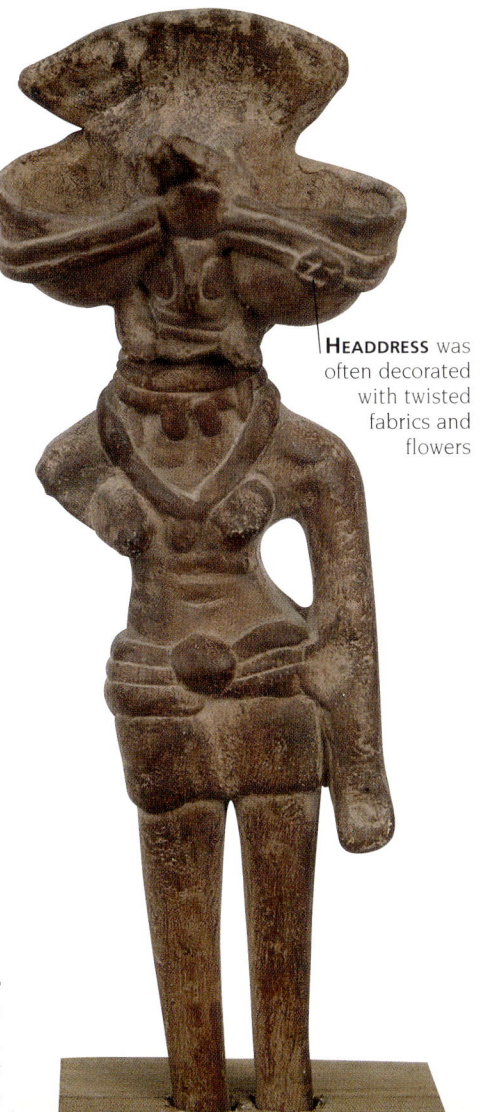

HEADDRESS was often decorated with twisted fabrics and flowers

POTTERY FIGURE OF AN INDUS WOMAN

INDUS WEIGHTS

▲ TRADE
The wealth of Indus cities came from crafts and trade. Craftworkers manufactured luxury goods, such as necklaces of pearls and carnelian, which were transported by merchants along the network of rivers. Imported items included silver and tin from Mesopotamia, and copper and lapis lazuli from Afghanistan. Indus people used a standard system of weights, based on units of 1, 2, 4, and 8.

DID YOU KNOW?
▶ Some time after 1900 BCE, the Indus civilization collapsed for unknown reasons. By 1800 BCE, all the main Indus sites had been abandoned. Buried under layers of silt, they were forgotten for more than 3,000 years. It was not until the 1920s that they were rediscovered by archaeologists excavating the Indus Valley.

MUD-BRICKS, which were the main building material, were first baked in wood fires or dried under the Sun

ASIA
Indian Empires

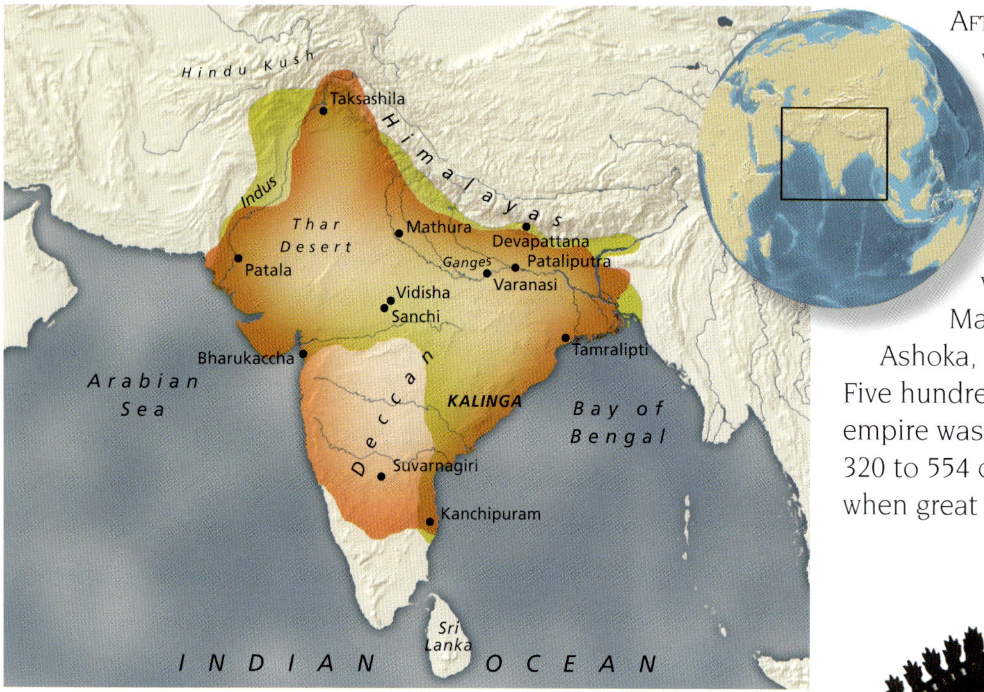

AFTER THE COLLAPSE of the Indus civilization, India was divided into small rival kingdoms. From about 321 to 185 BCE, India was united for the first time under the rule of the Mauryans. The founder of the Mauryan Empire was a nobleman and warrior named Chandragupta Maurya, who ruled from about 321 to 296 BCE. In the early Mauryan period, Hinduism was the most widespread religion in India. Later, Mauryan rulers, including Chandragupta's grandson Ashoka, were Buddhists, who spread the religion across India. Five hundred years after the fall of the Mauryans, a smaller Indian empire was founded by the Gupta dynasty, which ruled from about 320 to 554 CE. The Gupta period is often seen as India's golden age when great achievements were made in art, science, and literature.

THE MAP ABOVE shows the Mauryan Empire (brown) and the smaller Gupta Empire (green).

HINDUISM ▶

Early Mauryan rulers followed the Hindu religion, based on the belief that we are reincarnated after death, and our position in the next life is determined by the way we behave in our present one. The Hindu religion includes a huge variety of gods and beliefs. Over time, three gods came to be seen as more powerful than the rest: Brahma, the creator, Vishnu, the preserver, and Shiva, the destroyer.

HINDU GOD SHIVA

MAURYAN COIN DECORATED WITH STYLIZED SYMBOLS OF ELEPHANTS AND WHEELS

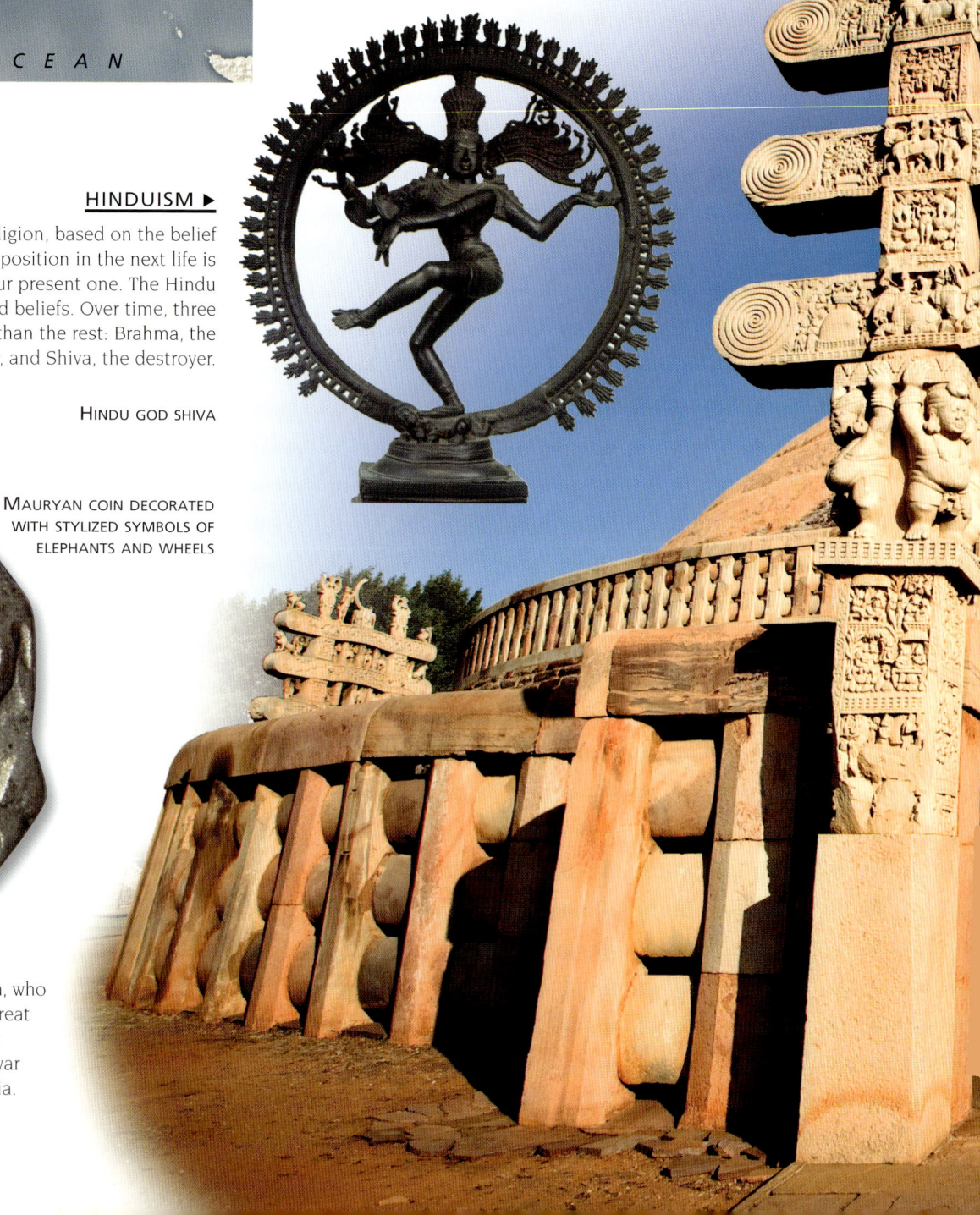

▲ THE MAURYAN EMPIRE

It is said that, as a young man, Chandragupta Maurya, who founded the Mauryan Empire, met Alexander the Great and was inspired by his example to become a great conqueror. Using an army of thousands of trained war elephants, he conquered the whole of northern India.

INDIAN EMPIRES

ASHOKA ▶
The third Mauyran king was Ashoka the Great (ruled 268–232 BCE). In about 265 BCE, Ashoka conquered the kingdom of Kalinga. Ashoka was so horrified by the suffering he saw in battle that he turned against violence and converted to Buddhism. He set up pillars all over India engraved with edicts (sayings). One edict described his sorrow at the suffering he had caused, and warned his successors not to make new conquests.

GUPTA COINS SHOWING IMAGES OF HORSES

▲ GUPTA EMPIRE
The Gupta Empire was founded by Chandra Gupta I (ruled from about 320–330 CE), who conquered the Ganges valley in northeast India. His son, Samudra Gupta (ruled from about 330–380 CE), continued to expand the empire, spending forty years conquering one kingdom after another. The Gupta Empire ended when the last emperor died in 554 CE.

▼ THE GREAT STUPA AT SANCHI
Ashoka spread Buddhism throughout India and sent missionaries to other countries, such as Sri Lanka. He also built thousands of stupas – sacred mounds holding relics of the Buddha and other holy men. These were places of pilgrimage for Buddhists, inspiring meditation and prayer. The most famous stupa is the Great Stupa at Sanchi, shown below.

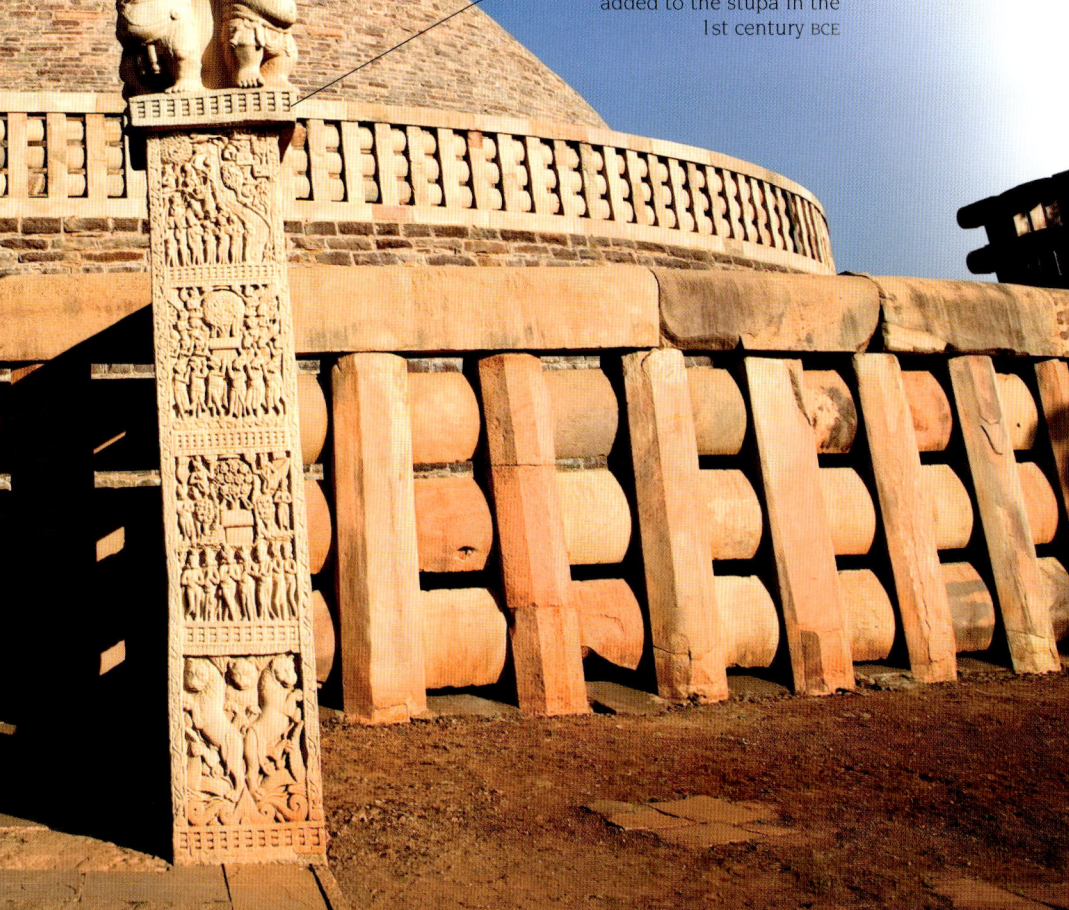

LION CARVING FROM THE TOP OF A PILLAR SET UP BY ASHOKA

DETAIL FROM A GUPTA CAVE PAINTING

▲ THE GOLDEN AGE
Gupta mathematicians were the most advanced in the world. They calculated the size of the Earth with great accuracy and invented the zero, making arithmetic much easier. Literature, music, and art flourished at the Gupta court, while the walls of many Buddhist cave shrines and temples were decorated with colourful frescoes, often showing scenes of the life of the Buddha.

STONE GATEWAYS, built in the style of wooden ones, were added to the stupa in the 1st century BCE

Siddhartha Gautama

Born into a noble Indian family, Siddhartha Gautama (c. 563–483 BCE) preached that fulfilment is reached through correct behaviour (dharma), and that suffering is due to human desire. If we conquer desire, we will no longer suffer. He dedicated his life to teaching and became known as the Buddha (the "Enlightened One").

ASIA
Steppe Nomads

THE STEPPES OF EUROPE AND ASIA form a vast treeless plain, with icy winters and baking hot summers. For thousands of years, the steppes have been home to nomadic peoples, moving from place to place with their cattle and sheep. Unlike settled peoples, who leave behind buildings, nomads left only their tombs. They also had their own religions, believing in a spirit world and worshipping the sky as a great father god. The steppe nomads were expert horsemen and fierce warriors, too. Steppe raiders, such as the Scythians and the Huns, were often a threat to the settled farming peoples of other parts of Asia and Europe.

THE MAP on the left shows the steppes (brown), which stretched for 4,800 km (3,000 miles) across Europe and Asia.

GOLD COMB DECORATED WITH WARRIORS FROM A SCYTHIAN KURGAN

▼ KURGANS
Nomads buried their dead beneath mounds called kurgans. Burials usually took place in summer, as the soil was too hard to dig in winter. Steppe peoples were buried with their belongings, including carpets, saddle covers, and even sacrificed horses. One kurgan, thought to belong to a powerful chief, contained the remains of 22 horses and 13 people.

▲ ON THE MOVE
The steppe nomads learned to ride as young children and spent most of their lives on horseback. They kept domesticated animals and used carts to transport their tents and other belongings. Skilled at working with gold, silver, leather, wood, and bone, they decorated many of the items they carried with them, such as their bow cases, horse harnesses, and combs.

BURIAL GROUNDS were sacred places

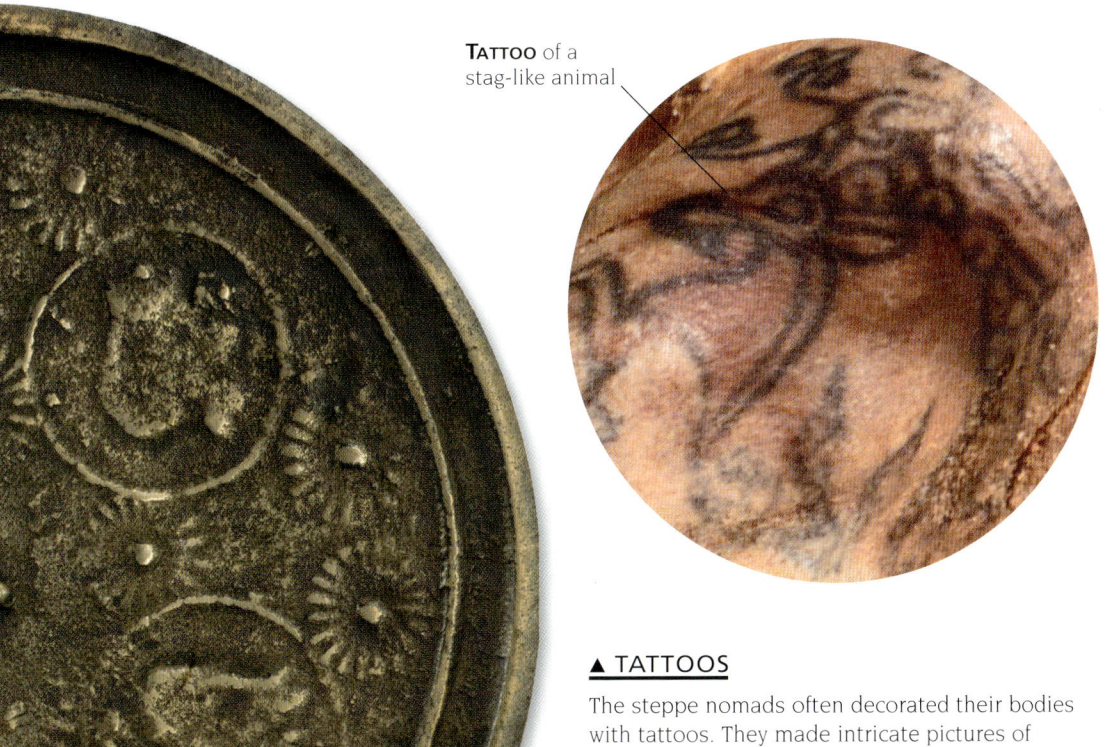

STEPPE NOMADS

Tattoo of a stag-like animal

Stag with its head bent back

SCYTHIAN GOLD ORNAMENT

▲ THE SCYTHIANS

The Scythians were a group of steppe peoples who lived north of the Black Sea. Much of what we know about the Scythians comes from grave goods found in their tombs. These goods included felt and wool items, colourful carpets, and many gold treasures.

▲ TATTOOS

The steppe nomads often decorated their bodies with tattoos. They made intricate pictures of animals and flowers by piercing their skin with needles and then rubbing soot into the wounds. The body of this young woman was preserved for hundreds of years in her frozen grave. The skin on her shoulder is tattooed with a stag-like creature, whose horns are turning into flowers.

MONGOLIAN SHAMAN'S BRONZE MIRROR

▲ STEPPE BELIEFS

Many nomads believed in a spirit world, and worshipped the sky as a father god and the Earth as a mother god. Some steppe tribes believed that people called shamans could heal the sick and communicate with the spirit world through trances. Mongolian shamans used bronze mirrors as magic armour to ward off evil spirits.

19TH-CENTURY PAINTING OF ATTILA LEADING THE HUNS

▲ HUNS

At certain times, several nomadic tribes joined together in huge mobile hordes. The most feared of these were the Huns, who invaded Europe in the late 4th and 5th centuries CE. Under their leader, Attila, they conquered huge areas of Europe and central Asia, and remained a powerful force until Attila's death in 453 CE.

DID YOU KNOW?

▶ Before the stirrup was invented in China in the 1st century CE, horsemen had to grip on to the sides of their horses with their thighs. It is thought that the steppe nomads were the first to wear trousers, designed to protect the legs when riding.

ASIA

The First Emperor of China

DURING THE WARRING STATES PERIOD, which began in the 5th century BCE, China was divided into several rival kingdoms. By 221 BCE, the king of the state of Qin had defeated all his rivals and formed China's first united empire. Taking the title of First Emperor, he set about imposing a unified way of life throughout China. He introduced standard weights and measures, and established a common currency and written language. He also built a defensive wall across the northern frontier and created a network of new roads. However, his rule was harsh, and the Qin dynasty was destroyed just four years after his death in 210 BCE. Yet, the First Emperor brought a period of stability to China and his influence lasted for centuries.

PORTRAIT OF THE FIRST EMPEROR PAINTED IN THE 18TH CENTURY CE

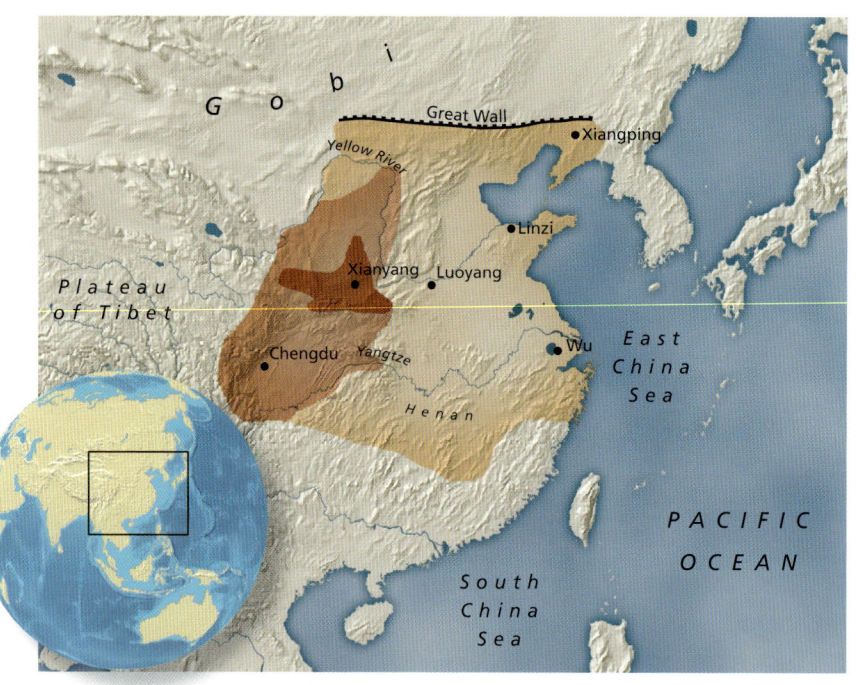

THIS MAP SHOWS the original Qin state in 350 BCE (dark brown), the conquests made by Qin rulers between 350 and 246 BCE (mid brown), and the conquests made by the First Emperor between 230 and 221 BCE (light brown).

▲ SHI HUANGDI

In 246 BCE, Ying Zheng came to the throne of the western kingdom of Qin, aged just 13. Between 230 and 221 BCE, Zheng led a series of campaigns against his rival kingdoms. In 221 BCE, he defeated the last remaining state and took the title of Shi Huangdi, meaning "First Emperor". The name China is thought to come from Qin (pronounced "Chin").

▼ STANDARDIZATION

To make it easier for people to trade across the empire, the emperor introduced standard weights, measures, and coins. His coins were circular with a square hole in the middle, which enabled them to be strung together. The hole also represented the Earth, which was thought to be square, encircled by the dome of the heavens.

CHINESE COINS STRUNG TOGETHER

CHINESE HORSE-DRAWN CARRIAGE MADE FROM BRONZE

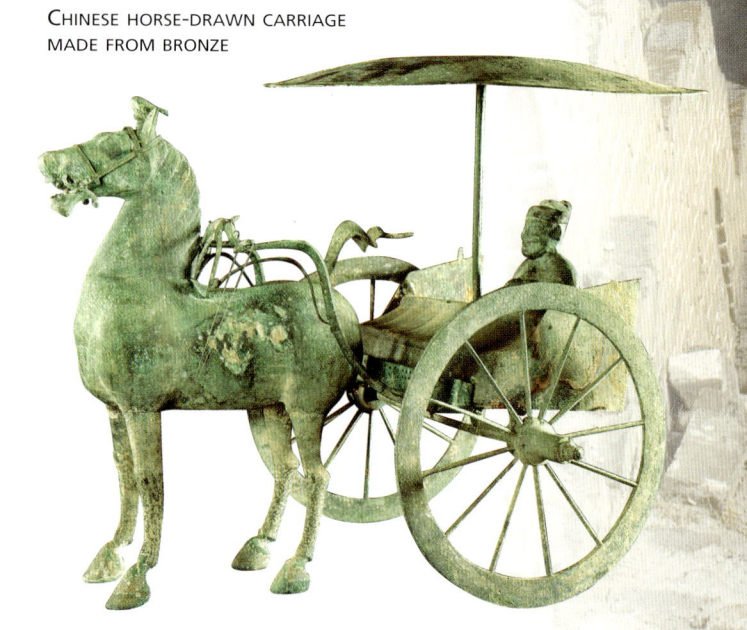

▲ ROADS AND CARRIAGES

Using forced labour, the emperor built a network of new roads that radiated out from his capital, Xianyang. He also built the Straight Road, which ran for 800 km (500 miles) from the capital to the northern frontier. The emperor standardized the gauge of wheels so that carts could cross the whole country using the same ruts, thus preventing the road surface from being worn away.

THE FIRST EMPEROR OF CHINA

WRITING ▶

Before the reign of the First Emperor, there were many regional varieties of Chinese writing. Shi Huangdi introduced a standard, simplified system, later called small seal script, which made it possible for the same texts to be understood across China. The emperor also imposed strict controls over what people could read. He ordered the mass burning of books that disagreed with his ideas, as well as the histories of the kingdoms he had conquered.

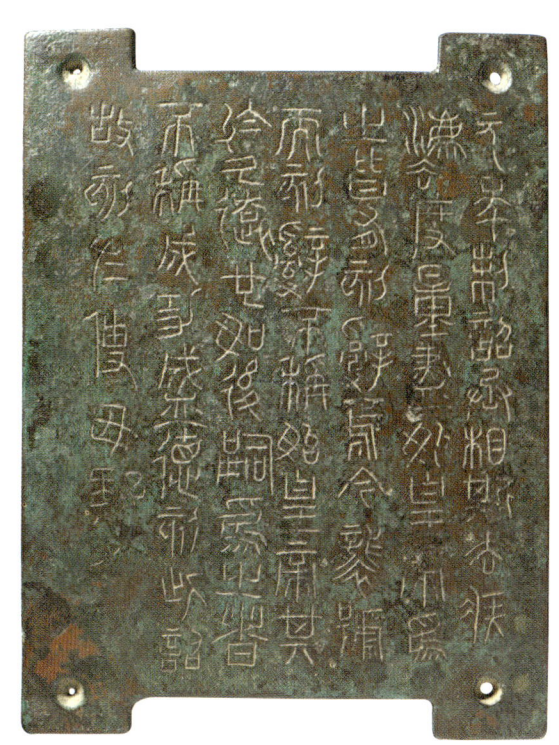

◀ THE GREAT WALL

In 215 BCE, the emperor sent 300,000 soldiers north to build the first Great Wall. Earlier states had created defensive borders to protect themselves from attack. The emperor knocked down all walls separating previous states, and joined the rest up to create a continuous barrier against northern raiders. The wall was rebuilt by later dynasties, and only a few traces of the original structure remain.

BRONZE EDICT WRITTEN IN SMALL SEAL SCRIPT

EACH SOLDIER originally carried bronze weapons

DID YOU KNOW?

Terrified of death, the First Emperor was obsessed with finding the secret of immortality. He believed that he could live forever if he found a magic medicine, called the elixir of life. His doctors prescribed so-called immortality pills containing large amounts of mercury. However, mercury is poisonous, and the emperor's pills probably shortened his life.

▲ THE TERRACOTTA ARMY

In 210 BCE, the emperor was buried in a vast tomb beneath a man-made mountain. Near the tomb were four pits holding an army of more than 7,000 life-size terracotta warriors, accompanied by 670 terracotta horses and 130 bronze chariots. Their role was to protect the emperor in the afterlife from the ghosts of the armies he had destroyed. The terracotta army was discovered by chance in 1974, during the digging of a well.

59

ASIA
China's Golden Ages

THE RULE OF THE Han and the Tang dynasties is often described as China's Golden Ages, when Chinese culture flourished and its people enjoyed long periods of stable government. The emperors of the Han dynasty (206 BCE–220 CE) created a professional civil service, with officials selected by a rigorous examination system. Rulers of the Tang dynasty (618–907 CE) were open to foreign ideas, and Buddhism, brought from India, became a popular religion. The Chinese led the world in technology, with inventions including printing, porcelain, and the magnetic compass. They also used the cocoons of moth larvae to make silk, which was traded across Asia along a series of trade routes.

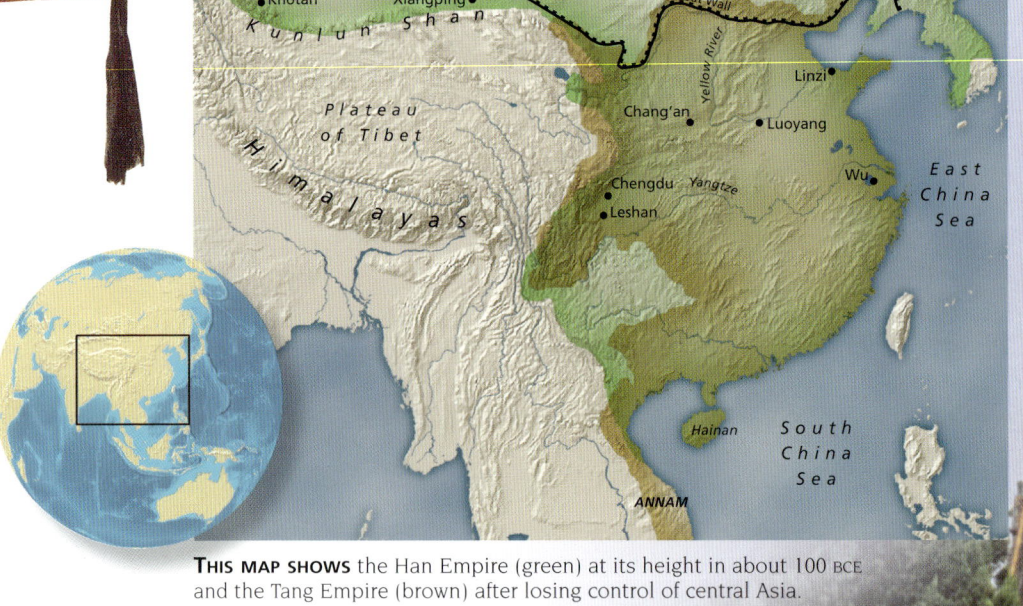

THIS MAP SHOWS the Han Empire (green) at its height in about 100 BCE and the Tang Empire (brown) after losing control of central Asia.

◀ TRADE

From Han times, China's main export was silk, carried through Asia to western Europe along trade routes known as the Silk Road. As China expanded under the Tang dynasty, trade increased. Thousands of merchants from all over Asia flocked to Chang'an, the Tang capital city. Chang'an had two huge markets, where Chinese silk, paper, and ceramics were exchanged for goods from all over Asia.

CHANG'AN ▶

Chang'an, meaning "Eternal Peace", was a rectangular planned city, built on a grid pattern. Unlike earlier Chinese rulers, Tang emperors welcomed foreigners, and many Muslims, Jews, and Syrian Christians settled in the city. The Koreans and Japanese were so impressed with Chang'an that they copied its plan for their own capitals.

PAINTED SILK BANNER FROM A HAN DYNASTY TOMB, DATING FROM ABOUT 168 BCE

CHINA'S GOLDEN AGES

BIG WILD GOOSE PAGODA – one of the few surviving Tang buildings of Chang'an

GIANT BUDDHA CARVED OUT OF ROCK AT LESHAN

◀ RELIGION

The Chinese followed three main ways, or systems of belief. Daoism taught that people should live in harmony with nature. Confucianism was based on the belief that people should behave fairly to one another. The third way was Buddhism, brought from India during the 1st century CE.

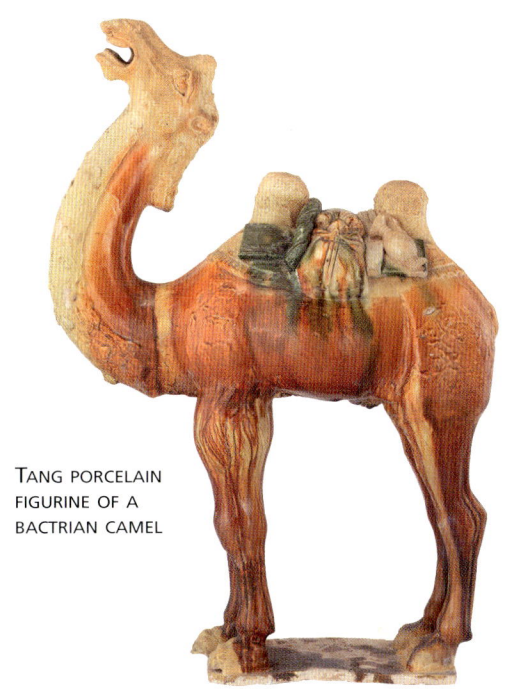

TANG PORCELAIN FIGURINE OF A BACTRIAN CAMEL

Empress Wu Zetian

Wu Zetian (625–705 CE) was the only female emperor in Chinese history. After the death of her husband, the emperor, she ruled on behalf of her sons. In 690 CE, she openly proclaimed herself the ruler of China. A Buddhist, she built many monasteries, winning support for her rule from the Buddhist monks.

▲ TANG ARMIES

During the Tang dynasty, China became a powerful empire. Tang armies conquered large areas of central Asia, where they used Bactrian camels to carry their supplies. They later lost these conquests, and the empire was further weakened in the 750s CE, when a general named An Lushan began an eight-year rebellion. Chinese armies were withdrawn from all foreign territories.

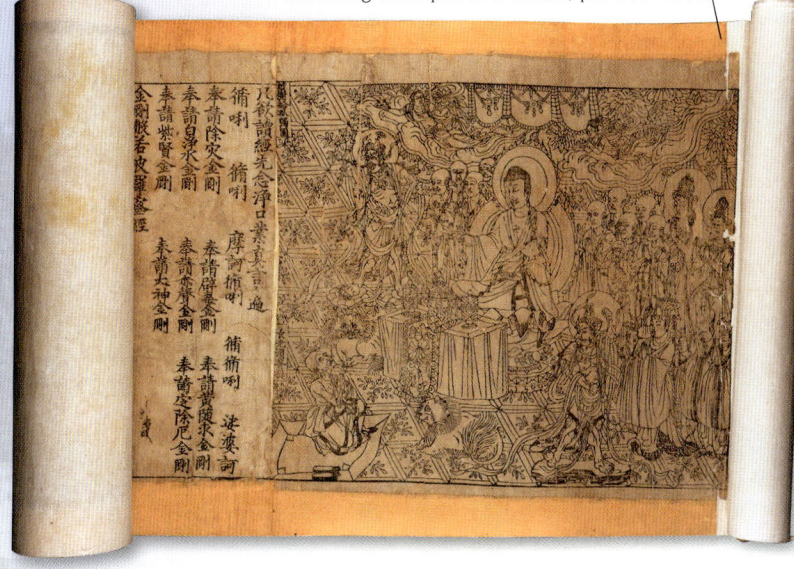

DIAMOND SUTRA, made in 868 CE, is the oldest surviving example of a dated, printed book

▲ INVENTIONS

The Chinese were more technologically advanced than any other people. Chinese inventions include gunpowder, the magnetic compass, paper money, the wheelbarrow, the horse collar, mechanical clocks, porcelain manufacture, and printed books. Printing was invented some time between the 6th and 7th centuries CE. The Chinese printed their books using carved woodblocks and rice paper.

ASIA
Korea

In 108 BCE, the Han dynasty of China conquered Korea. When Han power declined in the 1st century BCE, three rival kingdoms emerged in Korea. These were Koguryo in the north, Baekje in the southwest, and Silla in the southeast. There was also a small southern grouping of city-states, called Kaya, which joined together to resist their powerful neighbours. The period of the three kingdoms lasted from 57 BCE to 668 CE, when the king of Silla united the country. Early Korean religion had been based on shamanism, with its belief in a spirit world. Under Chinese influence, Buddhism was introduced, eventually becoming the main religion of Korea.

▼ BAEKJE

Founded in 18 BCE, the kingdom of Baekje was an important sea power with close links to Japan. Baekje was the most cultured of the three kingdoms, and during the 4th century CE, it adopted the Chinese script and introduced Buddhism. An alliance between Tang China and Silla led to Baekje being conquered in 660 CE, and its capital, Kongju, was looted and destroyed.

THE MAP ABOVE shows the three Korean kingdoms of Koguryo, Baekje, and Silla, together with Kaya, which consisted of a number of city-states.

ORNAMENT FROM A CROWN BELONGING TO A BAEKJE QUEEN

NOBLEMAN hunts with a bow and arrow

DETAIL FROM A TOMB PAINTING OF A KOGURYO NOBLEMAN

▲ KOGURYO

The largest of the three kingdoms was Koguryo, founded before 75 BCE. Merchants from Koguryo traded with China, exchanging furs, gold, and silver for Chinese silk clothing, paper, and weapons. Koguryo kings built impressive walled cities and palaces, and were buried in large tombs decorated with frescoes of mounted noblemen hunting deer, tigers, and bears.

KOREA

◀ SILLA

The most powerful of the kingdoms was Silla, founded in 57 BCE. The Silla capital, Kyongju, was modelled on the Chinese capital of Chang'an. Here, Silla kings were buried in heavily protected tombs under mounds created by heavy river boulders. As a result, the tombs were never looted and have been found to contain fabulous treasures, including elaborately decorated gold crowns. In the 660s CE, Silla made an alliance with Tang China, and conquered the other kingdoms.

CROWN was made of gold and only worn on important ceremonial occasions

JAR STAND would have held a bowl used to offer food to the dead person

DID YOU KNOW?

▶ Korean kings believed that they had to buy the land for their tombs from the Earth god. In 523 CE, King Muryong of Baekje was buried in a tomb, which carried an inscription saying how much the god had been paid. When the tomb was discovered, the coins were still in place.

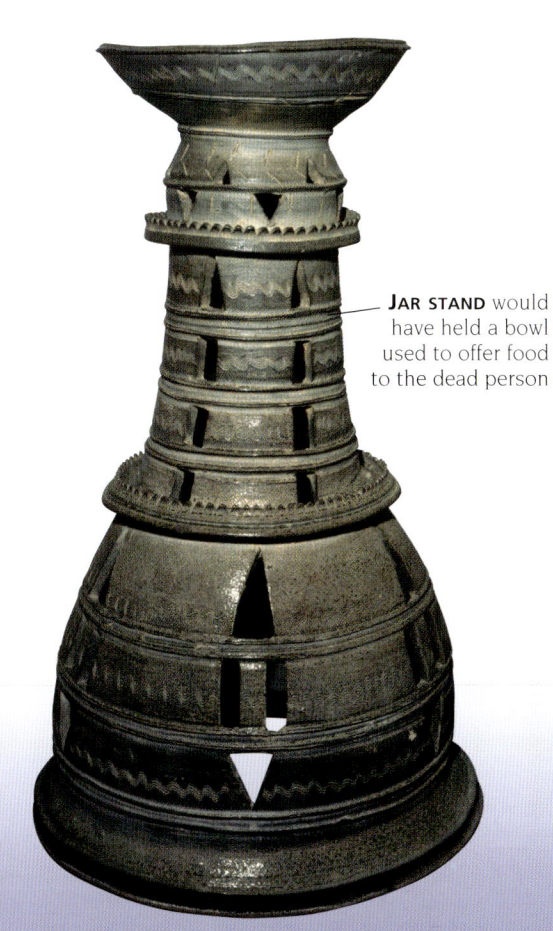

CROWN FROM A SILLA ROYAL TOMB

ORNAMENTAL JAR STAND FROM A TOMB

BULGUKSA BUDDHIST TEMPLE, BUILT BETWEEN 751 AND 774 CE

TILED ROOF, curving up at the corners, is Chinese in style

▲ KAYA

In the southern tip of Korea, a small group of city-states called Kaya flourished between 42 and 532 CE. The region had the best iron in Korea, and its people exported iron weapons and tools to Baekje and Japan. The tombs of the Kaya rulers contained offerings, such as this jar stand, and the bodies of sacrificed adults and children, who had been killed to serve them in the next life.

◀ BUDDHISM

Silla was the last of the kingdoms to convert to Buddhism. It was not until 527 CE that King Beopheung (ruled 514–540 CE) accepted the new religion. After conversion, Silla kings adopted Buddhist names and described themselves as "Buddha-kings". They built hundreds of Buddhist temples and had seated statues of the Buddha carved out of rock. Monks were sent to Tang China to be educated and to bring back holy texts.

ENTRANCE STAIRWAY has 33 steps, standing for the 33 steps to reach Buddhist enlightenment

ASIA
Japan

JAPANESE CIVILIZATION was greatly influenced by Korea and China. From the 5th century BCE, wet rice farming spread from Korea to Japan. By the 3rd century CE, a number of small states had formed. The most powerful of these was based in the Yamato plain, in the southeast. Between the 4th and 7th centuries CE, Yamato kings unified most of Japan. As they strengthened their power, they looked towards the Chinese court for a model of strong government. They adopted the Chinese script and Buddhist religion, which they promoted alongside Shinto, their traditional religion. In 710 CE, the Yamato rulers founded a new Buddhist capital, Nara, based on the Chinese city of Chang'an.

THIS MAP SHOWS the first Japanese states, which were eventually conquered by the powerful Yamato rulers.

◀ **LAND OF THE RISING SUN**
Yamato kings sent ambassadors to the Chinese court, and were impressed by the power of Tang emperors. While copying many features of Chinese government, Japan's emperors also claimed to be descended from the Japanese Sun goddess, Amaterasu, shown in this painting. She was important because Japan was the "Land of the rising Sun" – as the most eastern part of Asia, the Sun rose over Japan before anywhere else.

SUN GODDESS, Amaterasu, sending out rays of light

KEYHOLE TOMB of Emperor Nintoku was built in the 5th century CE

▲ **ROYAL TOMBS**
The early Yamato rulers were buried beneath huge keyhole-shaped burial mounds, called kofun, with the smaller graves of their courtiers around them. Thousands of pottery figures of warriors, dogs, and horses were included as they were believed to protect the tomb. The largest tomb belongs to Emperor Nintoku, which is 486 m (1,595 ft) in length.

RECONSTRUCTION OF AN ANCIENT JAPANESE GRANARY

▲ RICE FARMING

Most Japanese people were peasant farmers who grew rice in flooded fields. They grew rice seedlings first, which they planted in the fields. The water provided nutrients for the plants and prevented weeds from growing. The rice was then harvested and stored in wooden granaries that were raised on stilts to keep them dry and to deter rodents.

SHINTO SHRINE DEDICATED TO EMPEROR KAMMU (RULED 781–806 CE)

▲ SHINTO

The traditional religion of Japan, Shinto is based on the worship of spirits called kami. These range from small kami in rocks and trees to powerful ones, such as Mount Fuji and the Sun goddess. The Japanese built wooden shrines where they made offerings to their kami. Emperors, seen as living kami, also had shrines dedicated to them. Shrines have wooden gateways, called torii, marking a boundary between the everyday world and the world of the kami.

◀ CITY OF TEMPLES

Each of the first Yamato emperors founded a new capital when they came to the throne. In 710 CE, it was decided to establish a lasting capital, Nara, with a grid layout modelled on the Chinese capital of Chang'an. Nara was filled with Buddhist temples, and the monks played a big role in court life. This is the temple of Todaiji, founded by Emperor Shomu (ruled 724–749 CE). It was rebuilt in the 1700s CE.

TODAIJI TEMPLE was built using wood, and is still the world's largest wooden building

DID YOU KNOW?

▶ Japan has the oldest royal family in history. The present emperor is a direct descendant of the first Yamato emperors, who unified Japan 1,500 years ago. As the Japanese believed their dynasty was divine, no other family could take the throne. However, there have been times when the emperor was a figurehead rather than a real ruler.

Kingdoms of Southeast Asia

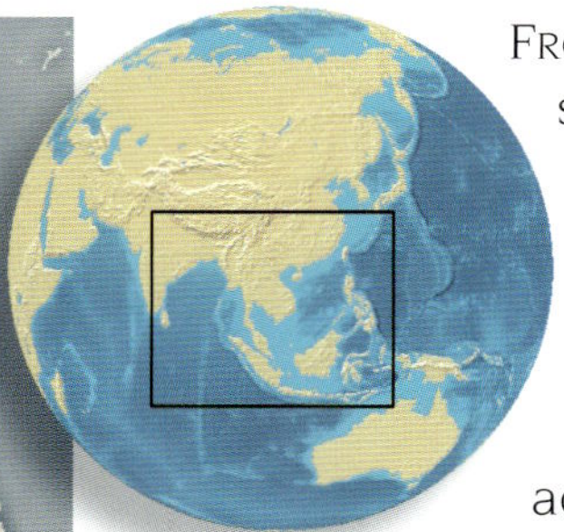

From the 7th century CE, several powerful kingdoms began to flourish in southeast Asia. While the island kingdoms grew rich from trade, those on the mainland drew their wealth from rice farming. The largest kingdom was the Khmer Empire, which included most of modern Cambodia and parts of Laos and Thailand. Its neighbours were the Pagan kingdom to the west, the Champa kingdom to the east, the Dai Viet Empire to the north, and the Srivijaya Empire to the south. Strongly influenced by India, the kingdoms adopted Hinduism and Buddhism, and built magnificent temples modelled on Indian architecture. The most impressive temple is Angkor Wat, built in the 12th century CE during the reign of the Khmer ruler Suryavarman II.

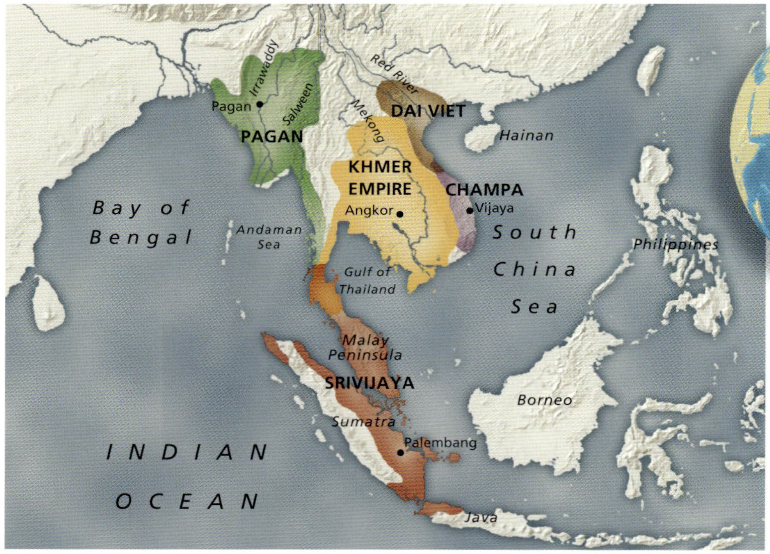

The map above shows the five major kingdoms of southeast Asia: Khmer, Champa, Pagan, Srivijaya, and Dai Viet.

◄ KHMER EMPIRE

Founded by King Jayavarman II (ruled 802–855 CE), the Khmer Empire flourished between the 7th and 15th centuries CE. Its royal capital, Angkor, had a large network of canals. These were used to bring water to the rice fields and to transport huge amounts of stone to build temples such as Angkor Wat. Khmer temples were modelled on Mount Meru, the sacred mountain home of the Hindu gods.

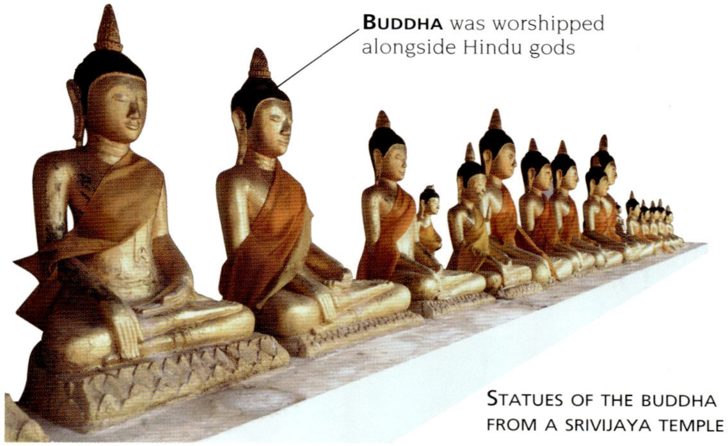

Angkor has colossal towers in the form of faces

◄ CHAMPA KINGDOM

East of the Khmer Empire, in what is now Vietnam, the Champa kingdom lasted from the 7th to the 15th centuries CE. Its people, the Cham, were traders who settled along the coasts where they built distinctive brick towers. Enemies of the Khmer, the Cham were fierce warriors who rode elephants into battle. Champa was taken over by the powerful Dai Viet Empire in 1471 CE.

Champa tower of Thap Poshaknu

PAGAN KINGDOM ►

From the 11th to the 14th centuries CE, Pagan was the capital of the first Burmese kingdom. Though smaller than Angkor, Pagan was the greatest Buddhist centre in southeast Asia. Its kings built hundreds of Buddhist monasteries and stupas (sacred monuments), as well as almost a thousand temples. Like the Khmer rulers, Pagan kings became wealthy through rice farming.

Dhammayangyi Pahto, Pagan's largest Buddhist temple

▲ SRIVIJAYA EMPIRE

The Srivijaya Empire flourished between the 7th and 13th centuries CE. The empire included Sumatra, the Malay Peninsula, and parts of Java and Borneo. The sea port of Palembang was the capital of the empire, which controlled the overseas trade routes. Like other southeast Asian kingdoms, the empire adopted Buddhism.

Buddha was worshipped alongside Hindu gods

Statues of the Buddha from a Srivijaya temple

DID YOU KNOW?

Satellite photography has revealed that Angkor, built in the early 12th century CE, was the largest city in the world before modern times. It covered 1,000 sq km (386 sq miles) and was similar in size to Los Angeles in the USA.

ANGKOR WAT

King Suryavarman II built Angkor Wat both as a temple to the Hindu god Vishnu and as his own tomb. After death, the king was believed to become one with Vishnu and would continue to watch over his people.

① The central tower, which stands on a raised terrace, is 213 m (699 ft) high.

② A stone statue of Vishnu stood in the temple's central shrine.

③ The inner core of the building was made from a coarse stone called laterite.

④ One of the temple's five towers – these represent the five peaks of Mount Meru (home of the Hindu gods).

The Americas

Some time before 16000 BCE, groups of hunter-gatherers crossed a land bridge from east Asia to the Americas. Then, the sea levels rose and covered the bridge, cutting off contact between the Old World (Eurasia and Africa) and the New World (America). Though the two worlds were separate from each other, their civilizations evolved in similar ways. As people began farming the land, complex societies formed. Like the peoples of the Old World, Americans had kings, organized religion, and temples. However, there were also differences between the two worlds. Americans did not learn to use any metals harder than copper. They had no animals strong enough to pull carts, so there was no wheeled transport.

76–77 The Aztec Empire
The Aztecs of Mexico were fierce warriors who conquered a large Mesoamerican empire in the 15th century CE.

Aztec warrior's feathered shield

78–79 Ancient South America
Civilizations also developed along the west coast of South America. The people here made beautiful textiles, using cotton and alpaca wool.

Figure from a cloth woven by the Paracas people in about 500 BCE

80–81 The Inca Empire
From 1430 to 1527 CE, the Inca people lived in the Andes Mountains of Peru. Here, they ruled the biggest and best organized empire of all.

Inca city of Machu Picchu, high in the Andes Mountains

82–83 Mound Builders
Farming spread from Mesoamerica to North America. The people built settlements with large earth mounds, serving as platforms for tombs and temples.

Hopewell pipe decorated with a frog

84–85 Pueblo Farmers
From about 300 CE, people settled in farming villages in the dry southwest region of North America.

Farmers growing maize

70–71 Early Mesoamerica
The Olmecs were the first American civilization, lasting from about 1200 to 100 BCE. They were followed by many later civilizations in Mesoamerica (middle America).

Colossal Olmec carving of a ruler or ancestor

72–73 The Maya
Eastern Mesoamerica was the homeland of the Maya, who lived in many rival kingdoms and often went to war with each other. The Maya civilization was at its height from 250 to 900 CE.

Maya vessel showing a king receiving tribute

74–75 Maya Beliefs
The Maya performed bloodletting rituals for their gods. They also viewed science and art as having a religious purpose.

Maya religious book written on fig-tree bark paper

Map: Pre-Columbian Cultures of the Americas

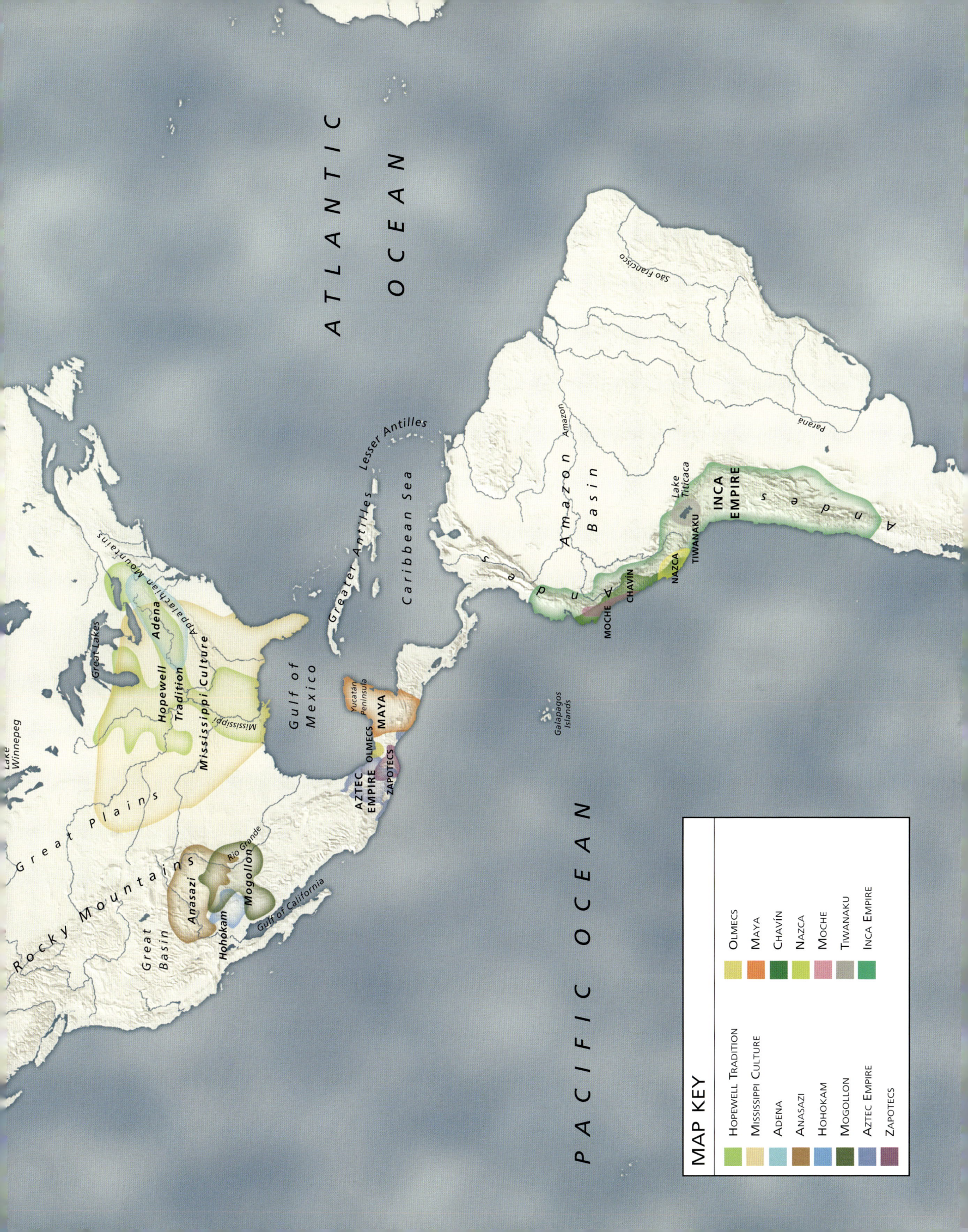

Labels on map:

- ATLANTIC OCEAN
- PACIFIC OCEAN
- Lake Winnepeg
- Great Lakes
- Appalachian Mountains
- Rocky Mountains
- Great Plains
- Great Basin
- Mississippi
- Gulf of Mexico
- Gulf of California
- Rio Grande
- Greater Antilles
- Lesser Antilles
- Caribbean Sea
- Yucatán Peninsula
- Galápagos Islands
- Amazon Basin
- Amazon
- São Francisco
- Paraná
- Andes
- Lake Titicaca

Culture areas labeled:

- Hopewell Tradition
- Adena
- Mississippi Culture
- Anasazi
- Hohokam
- Mogollon
- Aztec Empire
- Olmecs
- Zapotecs
- Maya
- Chavín
- Moche
- Nazca
- Tiwanaku
- Inca Empire

MAP KEY

- Olmecs
- Maya
- Chavín
- Nazca
- Moche
- Tiwanaku
- Inca Empire
- Hopewell Tradition
- Mississippi Culture
- Adena
- Anasazi
- Hohokam
- Mogollon
- Aztec Empire
- Zapotecs

THE AMERICAS
Early Mesoamerica

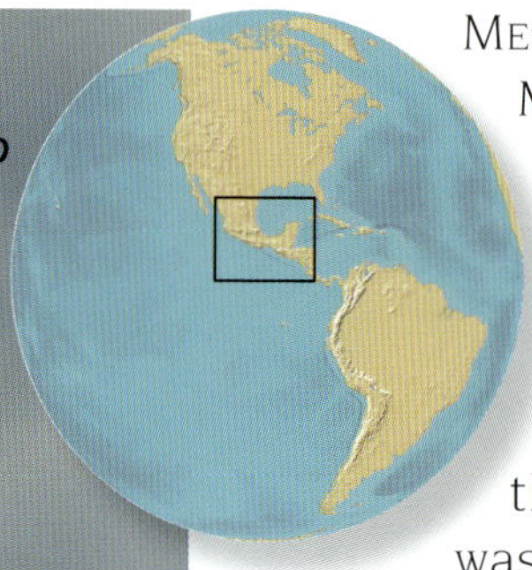

MESOAMERICA IS THE REGION running from central Mexico in the north, down to Guatemala in the south. From about 1200 BCE to the 1500s CE, there was a series of Mesoamerican civilizations, sharing common features – the people were ruled by kings, built towns with pyramid temples, worshipped similar gods, and played the same sacred ballgame. A widely held belief was that the gods had used their own blood to create life, and that humans should give them blood in return. From the time of the Olmecs, the very first American civilization, people drew their own blood to offer the gods. Mesoamerican peoples also went to war for a ready supply of prisoners to sacrifice.

THE MAP ABOVE shows the extent of the Zapotec and Olmec civilizations, together with the Mesoamerican cities of Tula and Teotihuacán.

ZAPOTEC CARVING

THE OLMECS ▶
Between about 1200 and 100 BCE, the jungles of the north coast of Mexico were the home of the Olmecs. These people built temple complexes, though little remains of their earth-and-timber buildings. They made huge carved heads, which may represent a ruler or an ancestor, and there is also evidence that they practised bloodletting.

▼ SACRED BALLGAME
All Mesoamerican peoples played a sacred ballgame in specially built walled courts. Players, who wore protective clothing, drove a hard rubber ball from one end of the court to the other, using their elbows and thighs. The game served a religious purpose, though this varied from one civilization to another. Losers may have been sacrificed to the gods.

OLMEC CARVED HEAD

▲ THE ZAPOTECS
The oldest surviving city in the Americas is the Zapotec capital Monte Albán, founded in southern Mexico in about 500 BCE. The Zapotecs were warriors, who made hundreds of stone carvings between 350 and 200 BCE, showing dead prisoners of war. Many of the figures have a picture sign – this may have been the name of the town. These signs form one of the first Mesoamerican writing systems.

BALL COURT OF THE ZAPOTEC CAPITAL, MONTE ALBÁN

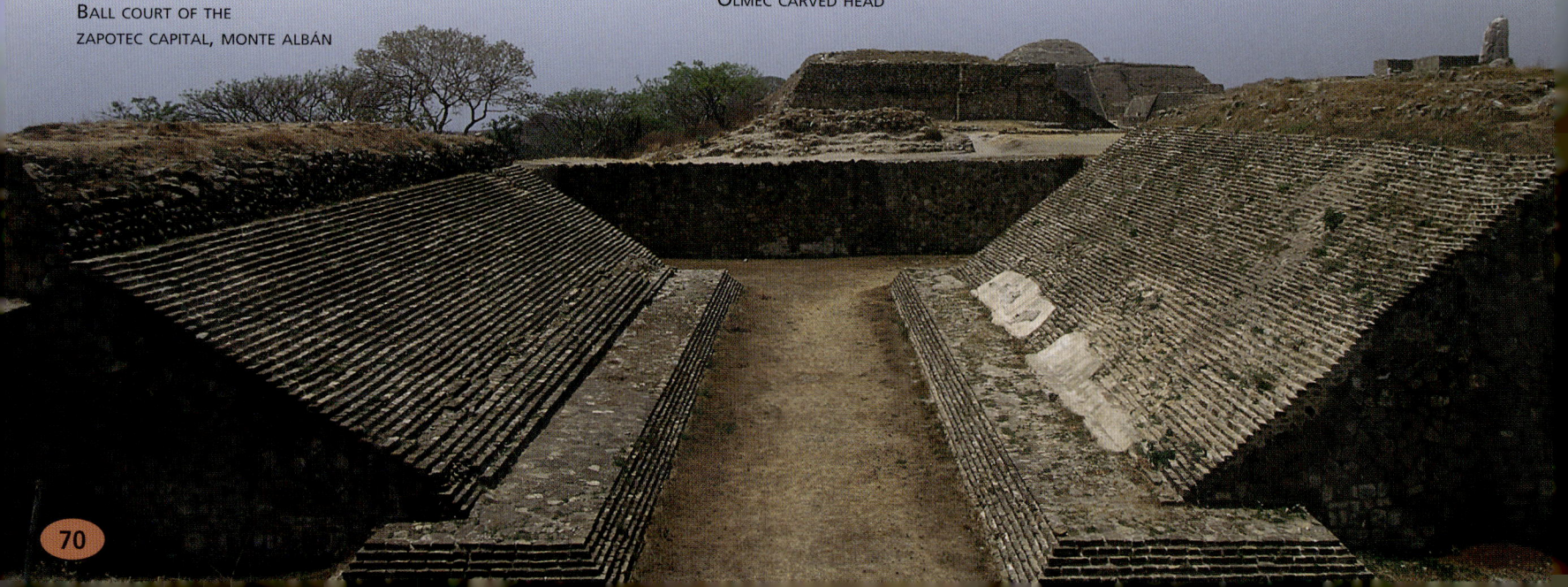

EARLY MESOAMERICA

◀ TEOTIHUACÁN

The biggest Mesoamerican city was Teotihuacán in Mexico, which lasted from about 150 BCE to 750 CE. At its height, in 500 CE, it was the sixth largest city in the world, with a population of between 150,000 and 200,000 people. It is possible that Teotihuacán was the capital of an empire, though we do not know how big this was. Two vast pyramids dominated Teotihuacán, which served as temples to the gods.

PYRAMID OF THE SUN AT TEOTIHUACÁN

BUTTERFLIES often appear in Mesoamerican art, linked with warfare

▲ GODS

For thousands of years, Mesoamerican people worshipped similar gods, though their roles changed over time. One important god was a feathered serpent, worshipped from at least 800 BCE. At Teotihuacán, he was a god who brought water to make crops grow. The Toltecs saw him as a protector of warriors. To the later Aztecs, who called him Quetzalcoatl, he was a wind god.

STONE CARVING OF THE FEATHERED SERPENT GOD FROM TEOTIHUACÁN

THE TOLTECS ▶

From about 950 to 1150 CE, Tula, capital of the Toltecs, was the most powerful city in northern Mexico. It was also the largest Mexican city at the time, but only had a population of about 50,000 people. The Toltecs were warriors, who sacrificed prisoners to their gods. The later Aztecs believed that the Toltecs were superhuman beings, who invented all the arts and crafts, and ruled a great empire.

DID YOU KNOW?

▶ The names we use for early Mesoamerican civilizations are those used in the 16th century CE by the Aztecs. They were so impressed by ruins of Teotihuacán that they gave it its name, meaning "the place where the gods were born". We do not know what the people of Teotihuacán called their city.

STONE PILLARS in the form of warriors were carved by the Toltecs

THE AMERICAS
The Maya

THE EAST OF MESOAMERICA, which is mostly rainforest, was home to the people known as the Maya. The Maya lived in numerous rival kingdoms, each with its own ruler and city. The cities, such as Tikal, contained spectacular buildings, including pyramid temples and palaces. Maya kings were constantly at war with each other, fighting for tribute and prisoners to sacrifice to the gods. The Maya civilization began about 800 BCE and reached a peak between 250 and 900 CE. In the late 800s CE, many cities were mysteriously abandoned and taken over by rainforests. However, in the south and far north, Maya kings continued to rule until the 1500s CE.

THE MAP ABOVE shows the extent of Maya territory (orange) between 300 and 850 CE, together with the most important Maya cities.

▼ MAYA CITIES

Every Maya city had a ceremonial centre, with stone palaces, ballcourts, and pyramids. Maya pyramids had stepped sides built of stone, and served as both temples and royal tombs. The largest Maya city was Tikal, which covered 60 sq km (23 sq miles) and was once home to between 50,000 and 100,000 people. The greater part of the city, where the ordinary people lived in simple houses, is now covered by rainforest.

KINGS ▶

A Maya king was also the chief priest and war leader. His role was to perform religious ceremonies to ensure that the rains came and crops grew. Many kings built spectacular monuments decorated with elaborate carvings and paintings. Every five years, King 18 Rabbit of Copán (ruled 695–738 CE) set up a monument, called a stone tree, that combined his portrait with descriptions of the ceremonies he had performed.

STONE CARVING OF KING 18 RABBIT

RUINS OF TIKAL, WITH ONE OF ITS FIVE TALL PYRAMID TEMPLES

TEMPLE is 44 m (144 ft) high, and was used as a royal tomb

WALL PAINTING SHOWING MAYA WARRIORS IN BATTLE

▲ WAR

Maya cities often went to war with each other. Warriors wore elaborate headdresses, decorated with images of gods and sacred animals. They were armed with clubs and spears tipped with razor-sharp blades of obsidian, a type of volcanic glass. The king led the army himself in order to capture prisoners with his own hands.

◀ PRISONERS

One of the main purposes of war was to take prisoners, who were sacrificed and their blood offered to the gods. Captured kings, whose blood was more precious than anyone else's, were not killed. They might be held captive for years so that their blood could be offered regularly to the gods. The Maya marked every important event with a bloodletting ceremony.

KING BIRD JAGUAR of Yaxchilán stands over a captive, who has been bled

MAIZE was made into tortillas and porridge

KING points to a pile of cloth and food that has been presented to him

STONE RELIEF FROM A SERIES OF CARVINGS MADE TO MARK THE ACCESSION OF BIRD JAGUAR TO THE THRONE IN 752 CE

▲ TRIBUTE

Maya kings did not try to rule the cities they attacked. Instead, defeated cities were expected to give tribute to the victorious king. This painted vessel shows a king, seated in his palace throne room, receiving tribute. Kings also received tribute from their own lords.

DID YOU KNOW?

Maya farmers grew their beans and maize alongside each other, a method that produces a better crop. The Maya would not have known that the reason for this is that beans add nitrogen to the soil, which feeds the growing maize.

▲ FARMING

The Maya used various methods of farming depending on the type of land. They cleared forest areas using stone axes. After burning the bush, they planted crops in the ashes. In swampy areas, farmers built raised fields, cutting canals and heaping up the earth. The main crops were maize and beans.

THE AMERICAS
Maya Beliefs

THE MAYA BELIEVED that their world was controlled by powerful gods. To please the gods, they performed rituals such as bloodletting. They were also the first people in the Americas to develop a writing system, and they were skilled astronomers and mathematicians, who invented complex calendars based on the movements of the planets. To the Maya, science and art served a religious purpose, and the planets and stars were seen as gods. Maya kings, who were thought to become gods after death, were buried beneath stone temple pyramids. The most famous royal tomb is the Temple of the Inscriptions at Palenque. This was the tomb of King Pakal the Great, who died in 683 CE.

◀ ASTRONOMY

The Maya were expert astronomers, able to predict solar eclipses and chart the movements of the planet Venus and the Moon. Venus was seen as a god of war – when it rose in the sky, Maya warriors set out to fight battles. There is evidence that some Maya buildings were used as observatories, such as this stone ruin at Chichén Itzá. It has openings that line up with positions of the Moon and the Sun at certain times of the year.

▲ WRITING

The Maya were the only people in the Americas known to have invented a complete writing system. They wrote using picture signs, called glyphs, which stood for sounds, words, and ideas. The Maya wrote books in coloured ink on paper made from fig-tree bark. The books, which folded up like a concertina, are called codices. The one shown above describes gods and rituals.

FLAMING TORCH held by King Shield Jaguar

MAYA QUEEN collects the precious blood

DID YOU KNOW?

▶ Inside King Pakal's pyramid, there is a small stone tube running from the burial chamber to the temple above. This was to enable the king's spirit to travel up to visit his descendants. The Maya believed that they could summon Pakal's spirit by offering him their blood.

▲ RITUALS

Maya kings and queens believed they could please their gods by making offerings of royal blood. This stone relief shows a Maya queen performing a bloodletting ritual. She pulls a thorn-studded rope through her tongue, and collects the drops of blood on bark paper. The paper would be burned, and the smoke would carry the blood to the gods.

MASKS ▶

Jade was the most precious material known to the Maya, and their kings were buried wearing jade death masks. Due to its green and blue colour, jade was linked with maize, water, the sky, and life itself. This death mask, belonging to King Pakal, was made of 300 jade tiles, mounted on a wooden frame.

JADE MASK was found in pieces and reassembled

THE TEMPLE OF INSCRIPTIONS

This temple was built by King Pakal (ruled 615–683 CE). His tomb was only discovered in 1948 by the Mexican archaeologist Alberto Ruz Lhuillier. After lifting a floor slab inside the temple, he found a stairway.

① The hidden stairway led down to Pakal's tomb, just below ground level.

② King Kan Balam, who has been offering his blood to his father, Pakal, walks down the steps.

③ Outside the tomb chamber was a box holding the bones of four men and a woman. They had probably been sacrificed to Pakal.

④ Pakal's stone sarcophagus had a lid with a picture of the king falling into the underworld.

THE AMERICAS
The Aztec Empire

THE LAST MESOAMERICAN CIVILIZATION was that of the Aztecs of Mexico. Between the early 1400s and 1521, the Aztecs conquered an empire stretching from the Pacific coast to the Gulf of Mexico. The Aztecs did not directly rule the peoples of their empire – they were allowed to govern themselves as long as they sent tribute to Tenochtitlán, the Aztec home city. The Aztecs practised human sacrifice on a larger scale than any other people. They were constantly at war, for they needed a supply of prisoners to sacrifice to their chief god, Huitzilopochtli. As a result, they had many enemies, such as the war-like Tlaxcalans, whom the Aztecs never conquered. When Spanish conquerors arrived in 1519, the Aztecs' enemies joined forces with them. By 1521, the Spaniards had conquered the Aztec Empire.

LAKE CITY ▲
Tenochtitlán, the capital of the Aztec Empire, was built on marshy islands in the middle of Lake Texcoco. The city was joined to the mainland with stone causeways that had two aqueducts, bringing fresh water. Within the city there was a network of canals, where people travelled around by boat. The centre of the city was dominated by a huge pyramid with two small temples on the top.

THE MAP ABOVE shows the extent of the Aztec Empire (purple), with Tlaxcalan territory in the centre.

FEATHER stands for 400 woven cloaks of this design

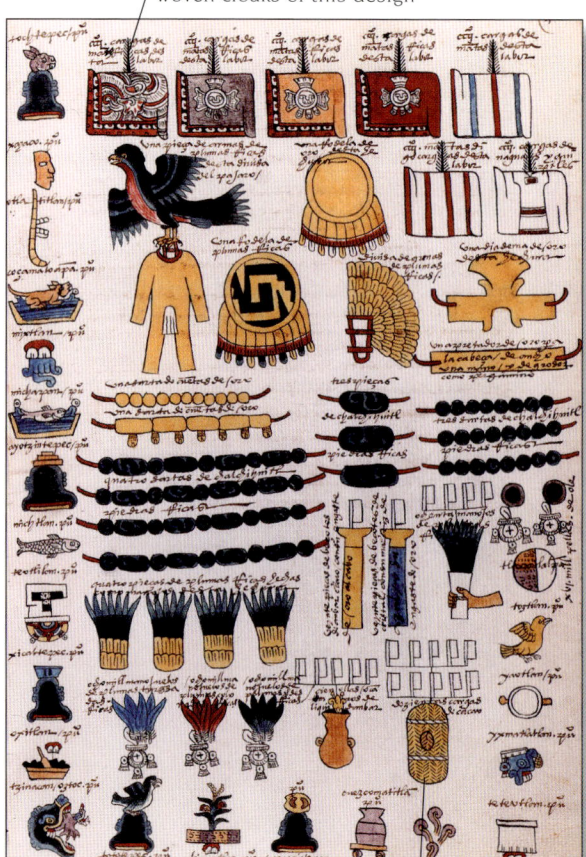

◀ FARMING
Aztec farmers grew crops on man-made garden plots, called chinampas, on the lake. They drove wooden poles into the lake-bed to form a frame. After tying basketwork to the frame, they piled lake mud inside. Trees planted around the edges held the soil in place.

TRIBUTE ▶
Conquered peoples had to send the Aztecs tribute in the form of luxury goods. The Aztecs kept records of the tribute. They used picture signs and a numbering system in which a flag stands for 20, a feather for 400, and a pouch for 8,000. This record shows the tribute from 22 towns, whose names appear on the left and bottom.

FARMERS build a chinampa

OVAL BAG with 10 flags represents 200 loads of cacao beans

THE AZTEC EMPIRE

CRAFTS ▶

Aztecs loved the brightly coloured feathers of birds, such as macaws and parrots, which they received as tribute from forest peoples to the south. Aztec craftworkers used the feathers to make headdresses, pictures, and decorated shields. The Aztecs prized featherwork more highly than gold. This shield combines feathers with jaguar skin, another item received as tribute.

GODS ▶

The chief Aztec god was Huitzilopochtli, god of war and the rising Sun. In Aztec art, he was shown as a warrior armed with a magic snake of fire. Huitzilopochtli shared the main pyramid temple of Tenochtitlán with Tlaloc, the rain god. For the temple's dedication ceremony in 1487, 20,000 prisoners were sacrificed at the top of its steps. Their hearts were cut out and burned as offerings.

AZTEC GOD, HUITZILOPOCHTLI

▲ SPANISH CONQUERORS

In 1519, Hernán Cortés led an army of only 500 Spaniards to Mexico. The Spaniards had better weapons than the Aztecs, horses, which the Aztecs had never seen before, and the help of local peoples who hated the Aztecs. At first, Cortés was welcomed by the Aztec Emperor Moctezuma. But after Cortés took him prisoner, fierce fighting broke out. By 1521, Cortés had conquered Tenochtitlán, which he rebuilt as Mexico City.

SPANIARDS in armour kill unarmed Aztec dancers during a religious festival

Hernán Cortés

The son of a nobleman, Hernán Cortés (1485–1547) was a Spanish conquistador (conqueror). At the age of 18, he set sail for the New World to seek his fortune. He arrived in Cuba, a Spanish colony, in 1511 and was appointed secretary to the governor of Cuba. In 1519, Cortés led an expedition to the mainland, where he learned of the Aztec Empire. Within two years, he had conquered the Aztecs.

THE AMERICAS
Ancient South America

In about 900 BCE, the first South American civilization appeared in Peru, on the west coast of South America. It is called Chavín, after its most famous site, Chavín de Huántar. The Chavín culture dominated the whole of Peru until 500–300 BCE, when it was replaced by several regional cultures. In the northern valleys were the war-like Moche, noted for their fine pottery. In the south were the Paracas, who wove beautiful textiles, and the Nazca, who created pictures in the desert. Further south still, the early empire of Tiwanaku developed in what is now Bolivia. Like the Mesoamericans, South American peoples were farmers, who grew beans and maize. They also grew potatoes and a crop called quinoa, which could withstand the colder temperatures of the Andes mountains.

CHAVÍN CARVING OF A SUPERNATURAL BEING WITH LONG FANGS

◀ CHAVÍN CULTURE
The people of Chavín de Huántar, in central Peru, built the earliest South American temple complex. It contained underground passages and ceremonial courts, and was decorated with carvings of jaguars, eagles, and supernatural beings. This same style of sculpture has been found across the whole of Peru, showing the widespread influence of the Chavín culture. The complex was abandoned some time after 300 BCE.

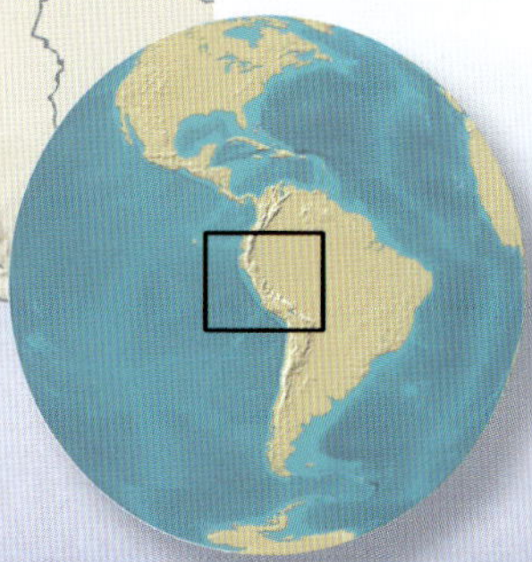

PARACAS PEOPLE ▶
The Paracas culture flourished from about 500 BCE to 200 CE on the southern coast of Peru. The Paracas mummified their dead, wrapping them in many layers of colourful textiles. The textiles were woven on huge looms and were richly decorated with human figures, animals, and mythical creatures.

THE MAP ABOVE shows the early Chavín culture and the later regional cultures of South America.

PARACAS TEXTILE SHOWING A MYTHICAL CREATURE

RUINS OF THE CITY OF TIWANAKU

ANCIENT SOUTH AMERICA

ELDERLY WOMAN is depicted carrying a heavy load

◀ **MOCHE CULTURE**

Northern Peru was the homeland of the Moche people from about 100 to 800 CE. The Moche were fierce warriors, who built large mud-brick pyramid tombs for their powerful rulers. They were also talented craftworkers, noted especially for their textiles, metalwork, and pottery. Many Moche vessels show scenes of warfare and daily life.

LLAMAS are still used for transport and wool

MOCHE POTTERY VESSEL

NAZCA FIGURE SEEN FROM ABOVE

▲ NAZCA PEOPLE

The Nazca culture flourished in southern Peru from about 200 BCE to 600 CE. The Nazca people were skilled craftworkers who made richly coloured textiles and pottery. However, they are best known for their vast drawings in the desert. By clearing away dark surface stones to reveal the lighter subsoil, they created patterns and pictures of animals and strange beings. The surprising feature of the pictures is that they can only be identified from the air – yet there are no hills nearby.

DID YOU KNOW?

▶ Llamas, the largest domesticated animals in the Americas, could carry loads of up to 60 kg (132 lbs). Yet they were not strong enough to pull carts, which may be why the South American peoples did not develop wheeled transport. Although they invented the wheel, they only used it to make pull-along toys.

▼ TIWANAKU EMPIRE

From about 650 to 1000 CE, the southern city of Tiwanaku ruled an empire that included all the lands around Lake Titicaca. At its height, the city had a population of between 15,000 and 30,000 people. At the centre of the city was a huge earth mound, topped by a stone court (shown below), where religious ceremonies were performed.

▲ TEXTILES

South American peoples kept llamas, alpacas, and vicuñas. The animals provided meat, dung for fuel, and wool. Llama wool, which is coarse and dark, was made into sacks, blankets, and ropes. Alpaca wool, which is lighter and finer, was made into clothes. The soft and silky vicuña wool was used only to make clothes for the nobles.

ENTRANCE to the temple court of Tiwanaku, guarded by a statue of a god

THE AMERICAS
The Inca Empire

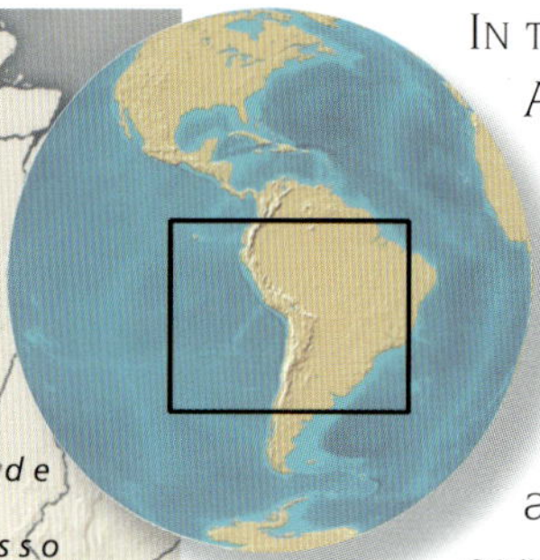

In the 15th century, the Inca people from the Peruvian Andes ruled over one of the most organized empires in history. It stretched for 3,500 km (2,200 miles) down the west coast of South America and included twelve million people who spoke more than 20 languages. At the very top of society was the ruler, the Sapa Inca. He controlled the lives of all his people, imposing taxes, forced labour, and compulsory military service. Inca men had to spend part of every year building roads, towns, terraced fields, and irrigation canals. Thanks to their vast network of well-built roads, the Inca people could organize and feed large armies, and send news quickly from one part of the empire to another. In 1532, however, the Inca Empire was destroyed by the Spanish conquistador Francisco Pizarro and his army.

The map above shows the Inca Empire (green) and the main road network (red).

◀ CHIMÚ EMPIRE
From about 700 CE, the Chimú people controlled land along the northwest coast of Peru. They created a powerful state, centred on the capital of Chan Chan. The Chimú were skilled potters, weavers, and metalworkers who produced beautiful artefacts in gold. The Chimú Empire was taken over by the Incas in the 1460s. Many Chimú goldworkers were taken to Cuzco to work for the Incas, who saw gold as a sacred metal.

Chimú warrior wearing a feathered helmet and ear plugs

Gold Chimú beaker

THE INCA RULER ▶
The Sapa Inca was believed to be descended from the Sun and was worshipped as a living god. He controlled the empire from the capital city of Cuzco. When a Sapa Inca died, his body was preserved by mummification. The mummy continued to live in its palace, where it sat on a golden stool. Each new ruler had to build a new palace.

Painting of the Sapa Inca Atahualpa (ruled 1532–33)

Inca quipu

▲ QUIPU
Although they had no writing system, the Incas were able to keep records on a device called a quipu. This was made up of a length of cord, from which other knotted strings were suspended. Detailed information was provided by the colours of the strings and the number, size, and position of the knots.

THE INCA EMPIRE

INCA TERRACES IN THE MOUNTAINS

▲ MOUNTAIN FARMING

Inca farmers grew crops, including maize, quinoa (grown for its edible seeds and leaves), and potatoes on steep mountain slopes. They created flat, raised strips, called terraces, by building long stone walls, and piling up soil behind them. Llamas carried vast quantities of soil up from the valleys, together with seagull droppings, which kept the land fertile. The Incas also built stone-lined irrigation channels to bring water to the terraces.

▼ MACHU PICCHU

Built in honour of the gods in the 15th century, Machu Picchu sits on a high ridge in the Andes 2,430 m (7,970 ft) above sea level. Situated between the peaks of two mountains, it contained farming terraces and hundreds of stone buildings. To the Inca, mountains were seen as powerful gods, who were the source of storms and life-giving rain.

▼ INCA BUILDINGS

The Incas built strong stone walls using huge irregularly shaped blocks. Locking together like pieces in a jigsaw, these fitted so exactly that it is impossible to slip a sheet of paper between them. Inca masons shaped these blocks using only stone hammers and chisels. Some of the blocks are 6 m (20 ft) high. Earthquakes are common in Peru, so the walls of the buildings had to be strong.

INCA BUILDING MADE FROM STONE BLOCKS

Francisco Pizarro

Born in Spain, Francisco Pizarro (c. 1476–1541) was a conquistador, hoping to find another rich empire following the conquest of the Aztecs. In 1532, with an army of less than 200 men, he attacked the Inca troops and captured their ruler, Atahualpa, promising to free him in exchange for a room full of gold. Once this was paid, Pizarro had Atahualpa strangled. Pizarro went on to conquer the Inca Empire, though he was later murdered by rival Spaniards.

MOUNTAINS surround the Inca city of Machu Picchu

THE AMERICAS
Mound Builders

The most fertile region of North America is the Mississippi valley of the eastern woodlands. From about 1000 BCE, people here hunted animals and farmed the land. They are known as the mound builders, because their settlements featured great piles of earth. The first were the Adena, a hunting and farming people. From 200 BCE, a wide trading network developed called the Hopewell tradition, with goods carried along the Mississippi and Ohio rivers. Almost 1,000 years later, farming had improved with new varieties of maize and beans arriving from Mesoamerica. This led to a rise in population and the building of the first true towns in North America. It also led to competition for resources, which caused wars.

This map shows the settlements of the Mississippi valley's ancient peoples.

Grave creek mound

Mound contained multiple burials

▲ ADENA CULTURE
The first mound builders were the Adena people of the Ohio River valley, dating from 1000 BCE to 100 CE. They hunted deer, elk, and other animals, and grew pumpkin, squash, and sunflowers. They built large conical burial mounds, including one at Grave Creek, which stands 19 m (62 ft) in height. New log-lined tombs and soil were periodically added to the mound.

Hopewell smoking pipe decorated with a carved toad

◀ HOPEWELL TRADITION
From about 200 BCE to 450 CE, a great trading network was created, stretching from the Gulf of Mexico to the Great Lakes. It is called the Hopewell "tradition" because many different peoples took part. Goods traded included obsidian, shells, sharks' teeth, and copper used to make jewellery, and animal and bird sculptures. Like the Adena culture, people throughout the region came to bury their dead in mounds.

MOUND BUILDERS

▼ MISSISSIPPI LIFE

The first towns of the Mississippi valley were built in about 700 CE and included flat-topped mounds. The people were farmers, growing beans and new types of maize imported from Mesoamerica. Farmers could now grow two crops a year, and support larger populations. The Mississippi culture spread across a vast area. Similar artefacts, like this copper portrait, have been found throughout the region.

Antlers were made of red cedar wood

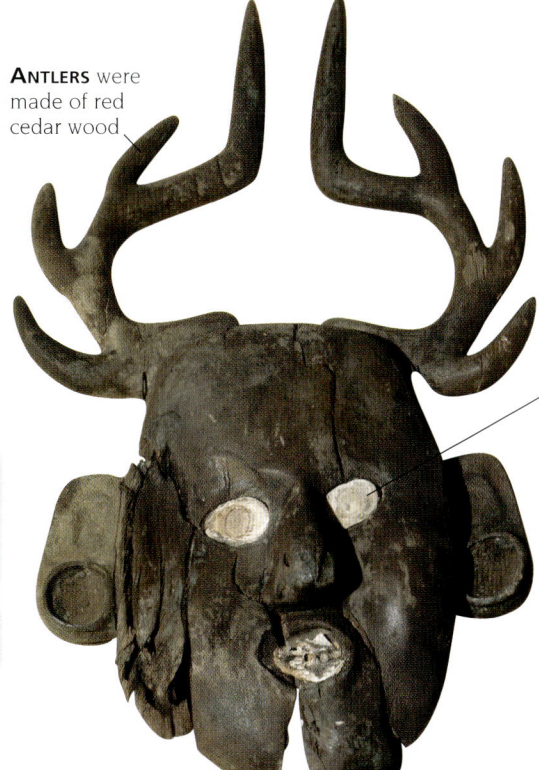

◀ GRAVE MOUNDS

Many mounds served as tombs, where important people were buried with offerings. Craig Mound in Spiro, dating from 1400 CE, had a burial chamber covered with human bones, and baskets filled with grave goods, including ornaments made of copper and shell. Among the offerings was this mask with deer antlers.

Shell was used for the eyes and teeth

COPPER PORTRAIT FROM A MISSISSIPPI MOUND

DID YOU KNOW?

▸ The Hopewell tradition was named after a mound of earth on the land belonging to a 19th-century farmer called Mordecai Hopewell. Similarly, the Adena culture was named after the Adena estate where another mound was excavated. We do not know what names these peoples called themselves, or what languages they spoke.

▼ CAHOKIA

The great town of Cahokia was founded where the Mississippi, Missouri, and Illinois rivers meet. It was home to 10,000 people and more than 100 mounds built from about 900 to 1500 CE. The biggest is Monk's Mound (shown below), with a height of 30 m (98 ft) and a base bigger than the largest Egyptian pyramid.

▲ WARFARE

As populations grew, there was greater competition over land and this led to war. People built timber stockades to defend their towns. Mound builders also made pots shaped like human heads with closed eyes, suggesting that they were dead. These may represent the heads of enemies. The lines on this portrait pot may represent tattoos, paint, or decorative scarring.

Mound once had a wooden building on top, which may have been the chief's home or a council chamber

THE AMERICAS
Pueblo Farmers

THE NORTH AMERICAN SOUTHWEST is drier and less fertile than the Mississippi region. Even so, people settled and found ways to farm. Their villages, built of stone or adobe (clay and straw), are called pueblos, meaning "towns" in Spanish. Three main groups lived in different regions. The earliest people were the Hohokam who lived in the deserts of the southwest from the 4th century BCE to the 15th century CE. The Anasazi lived in the northern desert from the 8th to the 14th centuries CE, while the southern forested highlands were home to the Mogollon people from the 4th century BCE to the 15th century CE. All were skilled craftworkers, making and trading pottery and ornaments.

THE PUEBLO FARMERS' TERRITORY covered much of present-day Utah, Colorado, Arizona, and New Mexico.

HOHOKAM ▶

The Hohokam people were resourceful farmers. They diverted water from the rivers to irrigate the desert. They built dams of wood, sending the water through canals to their villages. Sticks, stone axes, and hoes were used to dig the canals up to 3 m (10 ft) deep, and soil was carried away in wicker baskets. By 800 CE, they had the largest ancient irrigation system in North America.

HOHOKAM PEOPLE GROWING MAIZE BESIDE A CANAL

◀ CRAFTS AND TRADE

The Hohokam people made beautiful pottery and etched decorations on seashells, brought from the Pacific coast and Gulf of California through trade. The decorated seashells and pots were then traded for goods from other regions, such as copper bells and pyrite mirrors from Mesoamerica.

SHELL PENDANT etched with a pattern

PUEBLO FARMERS

Ball court was 30 m (98 ft) in length

RUINS OF THE BALLCOURT AT WUPATKI

▲ BALL COURTS

Like Mesoamericans, Hohokam people also built ball courts where they played a game with rubber balls imported from Mexico. Hohokam ball courts were located on routes between villages, and provided a meeting place for big gatherings. The largest court could seat 500 people.

▼ ANASAZI

The Anasazi lived in a dry region with occasional heavy rain in summer, causing flash floods. They built walls to contain and channel the flood water into fields. This is called flood water farming. The Anasazi lived in large, yet compact villages. Pueblo Bonito in Chaco Canyon had a network of rooms and underground chambers.

PUEBLO BONITO

RUINS OF CLIFF PALACE, THE LARGEST CLIFF DWELLING IN NORTH AMERICA

Round sunken room, called kiva, may have been used for ceremonies

DID YOU KNOW?

The Anasazi civilization ended in about 1300 CE. The cause was a mystery until scientists studied tree rings from timber found in Anasazi houses. These showed that there was a very long drought, with almost no rain at all between 1276 and 1299 CE. This was a disaster for a farming system based on rain.

◀ CLIFF HOUSES

In about 1200 CE, the Anasazi left their villages at the foot of Chaco Canyon and moved to settlements high up on cliff faces. They moved here for defensive reasons and to take advantage of the greater rainfall. They climbed up the cliffs using holes cut in the rock.

MOGOLLON PAINTING OF A BAT

▲ MOGOLLON

Like the Anasazi, the Mogollon were farming people, who used rainwater and flash floods to grow crops. They are best known for their art – images of dancing people, animals, and spirit beings, which they painted on bowls or chiselled on rocks.

Australasia and the Pacific

Unlike Eurasia, Africa and America, which were all linked by easily crossable land, the islands of the Pacific (Oceania) and the great continent of Australia had to be settled by sea. The settlement of Australia, before 50,000 BCE, saw the world's earliest known sea voyages. The people of Australia, called Aborigines, were hunter-gatherers. Much later, from around 1400 BCE, seafarers from New Guinea began to move out into the Pacific, eventually settling the widely scattered island groups of Micronesia, Melanesia, and Polynesia. Across Oceania, people practised horticulture, caring for individual plants such as breadfruit and taro, which they took with them on their voyages.

90–91 Pacific Voyagers

Polynesians, the greatest seafarers in history, crossed the Pacific in large sailing canoes, taking with them their families and possessions. As the population expanded on one island, they set sail to find new islands for settlement.

Modern Polynesian sailing boat

92–93 Pacific Peoples

Across the Pacific many different societies were created. In Melanesia, people lived in small tribes, while the Polynesians lived in larger groups and often went to war with each other.

Some of the hundreds of huge stone statues of chiefs and ancestors erected on Easter Island

88–89 Australian Aborigines

Australia is a hot and dry country. To survive here, Aborigines had to learn to live in the desert and semi-desert. They hunted kangaroos and other animals and gathered wild plant foods. Aborigines believed in a spirit world known as "dreamtime".

Aboriginal rock painting of a spirit being

MAP KEY

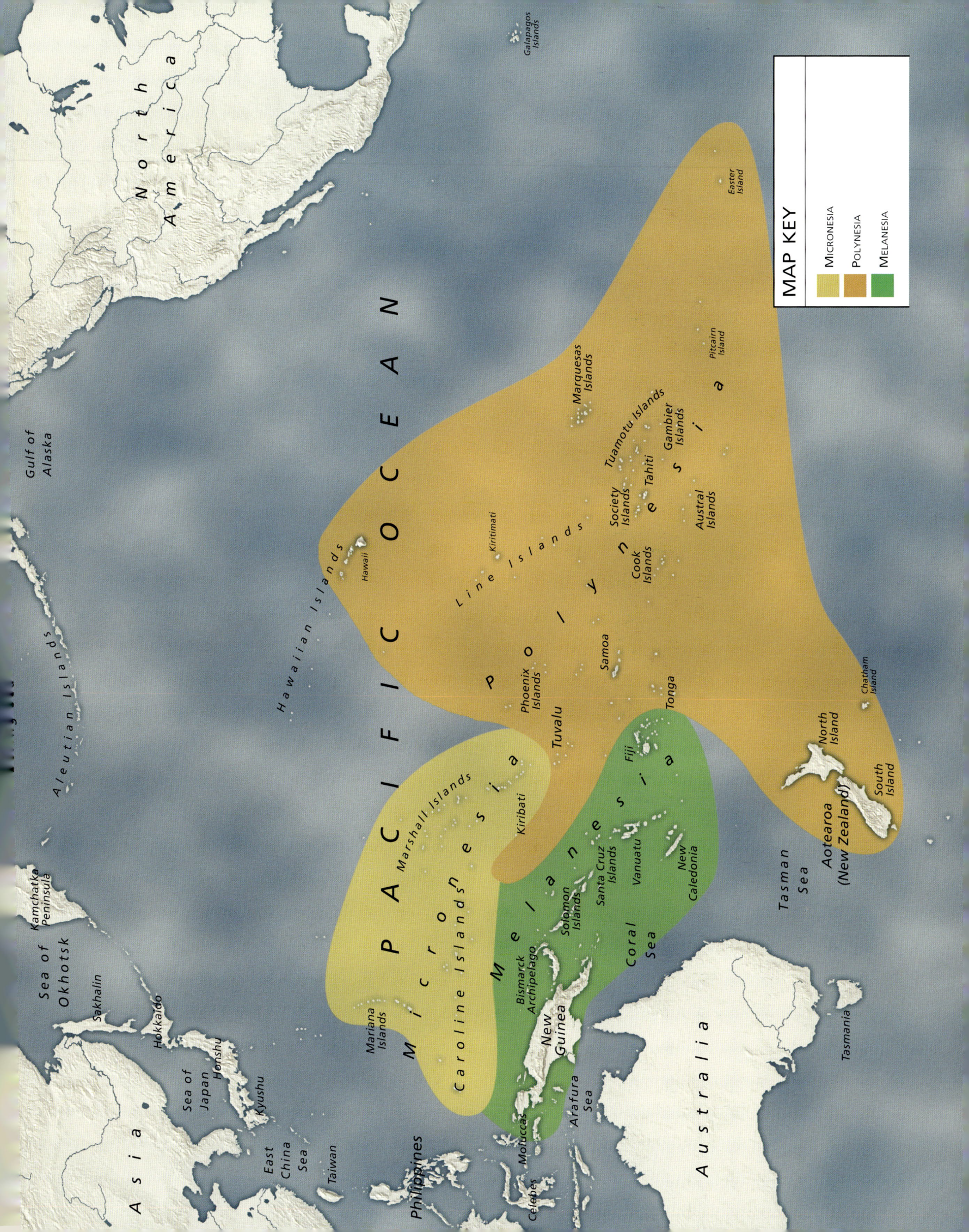

- Micronesia
- Polynesia
- Melanesia

AUSTRALASIA AND THE PACIFIC
Australian Aborigines

By 50000 BCE, even before our ancestors had entered Europe, we had crossed Asia and found our way to a new land, Australia. This was during the Ice Age, when low sea levels meant that Australia and Asia were closer together. Even so, the journey involved a sea crossing of more than 90 km (56 miles). In Australia, people had to adapt to the harsh desert and semi-desert surroundings. Living in small groups, the men hunted animals and the women collected seeds and roots. They believed in ancestral spirit beings who lived in a sacred "dreamtime", and held ceremonies in their honour. When the British settled Australia in the 18th century, they called the local people Aborigines, which is from Latin, and means "original inhabitants".

The red arrows show the routes of the first settlers into Australia, which was joined on to New Guinea at the time. Borneo and Java were also joined. Mainland Australia is shown by the blue dotted lines.

AUSTRALIAN LANDSCAPE

▲ DESERT LIFE

The main challenge of desert life is finding water and food because both are often hidden. People followed animals and birds to water holes, or ants to water supplies underground. They often had to dig with sticks to get to the water. Digging sticks were also used to collect edible roots and get animals out from their burrows.

BOOMERANG

▲ HUNTING

Men hunted many creatures, including kangaroos, birds, and lizards. Their weapons were wooden rather than stone-bladed and included spears with fire-hardened tips. To make their spears travel further, the men used a sling-like wooden device called a spear thrower. Its effect was to lengthen the throwing arm. They also used throwing sticks called boomerangs, which could kill small animals.

AUSTRALIAN ABORIGINES

WITCHETTY GRUB

◀ FINDING FOOD

Aborigines had to know how and when to find food. Many of their plant foods were only available at certain times of the year, and they often needed special preparation to make them edible. The knowledge was passed on by elders to the young. They learned that digging up the roots of gum trees could reveal witchetty grubs (the larvae of moths), which provide a good source of fat and protein.

DIDGERIDOO

▼ DREAMTIME

Aborigines believed that their ancestors shared the world with spirit beings, who lived in what is known as the "dreamtime". At the beginning of time, these spirit beings created the landscape and all life. Aborigines believed that the spirits and the ancestors could still be contacted. They painted pictures of the spirit beings on rocks, using ochre (earthy pigment) and clay. To the Aborigines, these paintings are sacred.

ROCK PAINTING OF A SPIRIT BEING

▲ SONGLINES

The spirit beings who created the landscape were thought to have crossed it following known routes, called "songlines" or dreaming tracks. Aborigines continued to sing the songs that they believed the spirit beings sang while travelling. During ceremonies, they performed dances, sang songs, and played musical instruments, such as the didgeridoo.

DID YOU KNOW?

▶ At certain times of the year, it was easy to find large amounts of food in Australia. November saw the annual migration of the Bogong moth. Aborigines gathered in great numbers to feast on the moths, which were rich in fat.

KANGAROO TEETH were used to make this necklace

▲ DRESS

Aborigines wore few clothes other than loin cloths. Bark, grasses, and human hair were all used to make different textiles. For ceremonies, they decorated their bodies by painting themselves with white clay, yellow and red ochre, and charcoal. Both men and women wore jewellery, including necklaces made from shells and the teeth of kangaroos and wallabies.

AUSTRALASIA AND THE PACIFIC
Pacific Voyagers

THE PACIFIC IS DIVIDED into three groups of islands. To the west lie Micronesia and Melanesia. The eastern group is Polynesia, a vast triangle of the Pacific Ocean, covering 25,000,000 sq km (10,000,000 sq miles). The Polynesians were the greatest navigators in history. While European ships rarely spent more than a day or two out of sight of land, the Polynesians were making sea voyages of up to 4,800 km (3,000 miles). Their expeditions were deliberately planned to find new homelands, and their canoes were laden with all the plants, animals, and weapons they would need. By 1100 CE, when they had settled all their islands, the Polynesians were the most widely scattered people on Earth.

BOATS ▼
Polynesian voyages were made in large sailing canoes with twin hulls of equal length tied side by side. Planks were tied together to make hulls and leaf fibres were woven into sails. A double canoe was about 30 m (98 ft) in length, and could carry 50 passengers, as well as animals and plants.

MODERN RECONSTRUCTION OF A POLYNESIAN CANOE

THIS MAP SHOWS Polynesia, a triangle formed by New Zealand, Hawaii, and Easter Island, together with the routes taken by Pacific settlers.

◄ NAVIGATION
Polynesians worked out their position by the rising and setting of stars, the movement of the Sun, and the direction of the wind and ocean swells. They could detect distant islands by the flight of birds, cloud formations, driftwood, and the changing colour of the sea. They may have made stick maps showing the islands and swells.

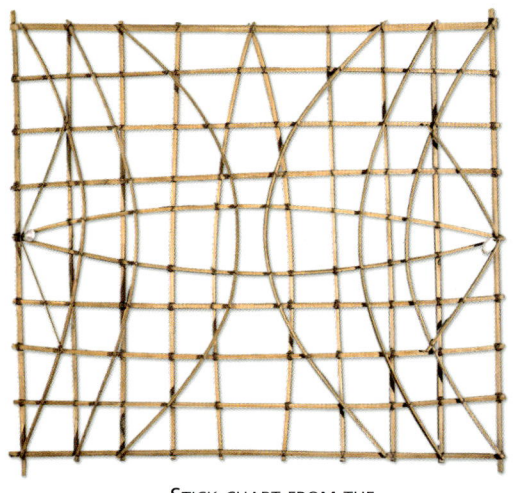

STICK CHART FROM THE MARSHALL ISLANDS OF MICRONESIA

PACIFIC VOYAGERS

BREADFRUIT was cooked whole in an open fire.

ANIMAL TRAVELLERS ▶

Polynesians took pigs, dogs, chickens, and rats on their voyages. These were successfully introduced everywhere except New Zealand, which had only dogs, and Easter Island, where there were only chickens. The dogs were fed on vegetables and used for meat. The pigs were good animals to take on voyages because they could be fed on human waste.

PIGS were the most prized meat source.

▲ HORTICULTURE

Polynesians were horticulturalists, growing plants that had to be individually cared for. Their main crops were breadfruit, bananas, taro, yams, sweet potatoes, and plantains. They carried all these plants on their canoes as small seedlings. The crops did well in the warm tropics, but only the sweet potato survived in the cooler southern lands of Easter Island and New Zealand.

◀ NEW ZEALAND

The last part of Polynesia was settled in about 1100 CE. New Zealand or Aotearoa (meaning "Land of the Long White Cloud") was larger than the rest of the Polynesian islands put together. Although their pigs and chickens did not survive the journey, the Polynesians found many large flightless birds, such as the moa, which were easy to hunt. The settlers, known as Māori, were expert wood carvers.

MĀORI WOOD CARVING

WARFARE ▶

Throughout Polynesia, warfare was common. Motives for fighting included the pressure caused by overpopulation, as well as long-lasting feuds. It was probably partly to escape the pressure of rising populations that Polynesians set off on their voyages. Prisoners were often sacrificed and eaten. In the Marquesas Islands, human flesh was a prized food called long pig.

POLYNESIAN WAR CLUB

DID YOU KNOW?

▶ The coming of the Māori had a devastating impact on the New Zealand wildlife. By the 1300s CE, all ten species of moa and many other types of bird had been wiped out. This was caused by hunting, forest clearance, and the arrival of rats, which ate the birds' eggs.

91

AUSTRALASIA
Pacific Peoples

PACIFIC PEOPLES CREATED different types of society. In Melanesia, people lived in small tribes ruled by "big men", whose power came from their reputation for wisdom. Polynesians lived in larger groups, ruled by chiefs, whose power was religious and inherited from distant ancestors. Chiefs had great power, receiving tribute and labour from ordinary people. They displayed their rank with tattoos and feathered collars, and wore beautifully carved jade ornaments. On Easter Island, people set up massive statues of their chiefs and ancestors. To the west of Polynesia lies Pohnpei in Micronesia, where powerful kings ruled from about 500 to 1450 CE from their capital, Nan Madol.

THE PACIFIC is divided into three large regions: Polynesia in the east, and Melanesia and Micronesia in the west.

▼ TATTOOS

The Polynesians used tattoos as a display of rank. The more elaborately a man was tattooed, the greater his prestige and power. Using small bone chisels, Polynesians made cuts on their skin, and rubbed soot into the wounds. In New Zealand, tattooed heads of dead chiefs were preserved as prized possessions by their families.

◀ CHIEFS

The Polynesian chiefs were thought to have supernatural power, called mana, inherited from their ancestors. To protect this power, there was a range of prohibitions called taboos. In Hawaii, it was taboo to touch the clothes or shadows of chiefs. In Tahiti, people could not say a chief's name. Even chiefs had to obey taboos.

FEATHER COLLAR WORN BY A TAHITIAN CHIEF

DID YOU KNOW?

- Easter Island people used log rollers to transport their massive statues from the quarries. In the process, they completely stripped Easter Island of its trees.

◀ ART

Although the Polynesians did not use pottery or metals, they were highly skilled in making works of art from stone, wood, shell, bone, and vegetable fibres. In New Zealand, Māori carved greenstone pendants, called hei tiki, and wore them around their necks. These were believed to possess magical powers, which increased as they were passed on from generation to generation.

GREENSTONE PENDANT

MĀORI CARVING OF A TATTOOED ANCESTOR FIGURE

STATUES are now almost all half-buried or toppled

EASTER ISLAND STATUES ▶

In eastern Polynesia, people built religious structures, with paved courts and platforms. On Easter Island, the platforms were the bases for 887 statues of chiefs and ancestors, set up between 1250 and 1500 CE. The statues originally had eyes made from coral and obsidian, and a red stone topknot.

NAN MADOL

Off the eastern shore of Pohnpei lies Nan Madol. Consisting of 92 artificial islets, it was divided into two areas. This is Madol Pah, to the southwest, where kings lived and carried out public ceremonies. To the northeast, there was the royal burial area called Madol Powe.

1. Ceremonies took place in the temple.
2. The children were taught by their elders, listening to stories that were passed down through the ages.
3. The dwellings were made of timber and had tall thatched roofs.

Glossary

ABORIGINE
A name used by British settlers in Australia to refer to the local people. From Latin, it means "original inhabitant".

AMPHITHEATRE
A large oval building for public shows built by the Romans.

ANCIENT
Belonging to the distant past.

ARCHAEOLOGIST
Someone who studies the past by looking for the remains of buildings and other artefacts, often by digging them up.

ARTEFACT
Any object made or used by people in the past. Archaeologists study artefacts, such as stone tools, to find out how ancient people lived.

ASTRONOMER
Someone who studies the movements of the planets, stars, and other heavenly bodies.

BCE
A method of dating. The abbreviation stands for "Before the Common Era", which covers the period of history before Jesus Christ was believed to have been born.

BRONZE
Metal made by mixing tin and copper. Bronze was invented at different times in different places, beginning in Anatolia (Turkey) in about 3500 BCE.

BUDDHISM
A religion and philosophy based on the teachings of the Buddha. Buddhism originated in India and then spread across east Asia.

BURIAL MOUND
An artificial hill of earth or stones built to cover a grave.

CE
A method of dating, which stands for the "Common Era". It's first year is 1 CE, which is the same as AD 1 in the Christian calendar.

CITY-STATE
A small state based on a city, which ruled the surrounding countryside.

CIVILIZATION
A society in an advanced state of development.

COLONIES
Settlements made by people who had left their homeland in search of new places to live.

CONQUISTADOR
A name given to a Spanish conqueror of the Americas.

CULTURE
A particular society at a particular time and place.

CUNEIFORM
Writing system of ancient Mesopotamia (Iraq). The name means "wedge shaped".

DREAMTIME
In Australian Aboriginal thought this was the time of the creation of the world by spirit beings.

DYNASTY
A family line of rulers.

EDICT
An official command, or law proclamation, issued by a ruler.

EMPIRE
A large area, with different peoples, under the rule of a single powerful state or people.

FERTILE
Able to produce new life. Fertile soil is good for growing crops.

HAN
The Han dynasty ruled China from 206 BCE–220 CE.

HELLENISTIC AGE
Period following the death of Alexander the Great in 323 BCE when the Greek way of life spread throughout the lands he had conquered.

HIEROGLYPHS
The name of the ancient Egyptian writing system, which used pictures of objects, animals, and people to stand for words, ideas, and sounds. It means "sacred signs".

HINDUISM
The ancient religion of India. It is based on the worship of many gods and a belief that, after death, we are reborn in new bodies.

HORTICULTURE
The care of individual plants. This is in contrast to farming, where large numbers of plants are grown together in fields.

ICE AGE
Cold periods in Earth's history are called Ice Ages. There have been four major Ice Ages in the past.

INCENSE
Sweet-smelling resin from trees, including frankincense and myrrh. Incense was burned as offerings to gods and used in perfumes.

IRRIGATION
The control of water for the purpose of farming. An example is the digging of a canal to take water from a river to a field.

LINEAR A
Writing system invented by the Minoan people of Crete. It has not been deciphered.

LINEAR B
Writing system, based on Linear A, used by the Mycenaean people of Greece to write Greek.

MAYA
The ancient people of eastern Mesoamerica. The Maya lived in many rival kingdoms and built tall pyramid temples.

MEGALITH
Any huge stone monument is called a megalith. Megalith means "big stone" in Greek.

MELANESIA
The islands of the western Pacific to the northeast of Australia. Melanesia, meaning "black islands", comes from the islanders' skin colour.

MESOAMERICA
A region stretching from Mexico in the north down to Guatemala in the south.

MESOPOTAMIA
The area between the Tigris and Euphrates rivers in what is now Iraq. The name, which is Greek, means "between the rivers".

GLOSSARY

MICRONESIA
A region of the western Pacific with hundreds of small islands. The name means "small islands".

MIDDLE EAST
The region of western Asia stretching from Turkey in the west to Iran in the east. Egypt is also often included.

MONSOON
A strong wind that switches direction at different seasons of the year.

NEOLITHIC
Meaning "New Stone" Age, when farming was invented. This period began in the Middle East between 10000 and 9000 BCE and ended with the coming of metal tools at different times in different places.

NOMADS
People who spend their lives moving from place to place, seeking pasture for herds of grazing animals. The name comes from a Greek term meaning "to pasture".

OASIS
A fertile area in a desert, where there is water allowing plants to grow.

PAPYRUS
An Egyptian water reed that grows on the Nile. It was used to make paper, a word that comes from papyrus.

PASSAGE GRAVE
A Neolithic tomb with a long stone-lined passage leading to a burial chamber.

PHALANX
A military formation in which warriors march together in close packed ranks with shields and spears. Phalanxes were used by the Greeks and the Macedonians.

PHARAOH
The title of a king of ancient Egypt. It comes from "per-aa", meaning "great house", and originally referred to the palace of the king.

PHILOSOPHY
The word philosophy comes from Greek and means "love of wisdom". Philosophers try to answer big questions, such as what is the right way to live?

POLIS
The Greek name for a city-state.

POLYNESIA
Region of the Pacific Ocean stretching from New Zealand in the southwest to the Hawaiian islands in the north and Easter Island in the southeast. Polynesia means "many islands".

PORCELAIN
A type of pottery invented in China. It was made by heating a special clay, called kaolin, to high temperatures in a kiln.

PRIEST
Someone whose role is to perform religious ceremonies.

PYRAMID
A large monument with a square or rectangular base and four triangular sides. Pyramids served as tombs in ancient Egypt and as both temples and tombs in Mesoamerica.

QIN
The first dynasty to rule all China, lasting from 221–207 BCE.

REPUBLIC
A state ruled by elected officials rather than a king.

SACRIFICE
A gift to a god. Sacrifices included animals and people, killed as offerings to gods.

SCRIBE
A person who writes or keeps records.

SEA PEOPLES
A group of peoples who invaded many lands around the eastern Mediterranean in the 12th century BCE.

SHAMANISM
A religion in which experts called shamans contact spirits.

SHINTO
The ancient religion of Japan. It is based on the worship of spirits called kami.

SHRINE
A place where holy objects, such as statues of gods, are kept and worshipped.

SILK ROADS
Several trade routes from China to the Middle East, named after the most valuable product traded, silk.

SILT
Fine soil carried by water.

SLAVE
Someone who is owned as property by another person. Slaves might be captured in war or born from slave parents.

STELE
An upright carved stone monument. Steles have been set up by rulers to honour the gods, to list laws, or to mark a tomb.

STEPPE
A flat, grassy, and treeless plain.

STUPA
A dome-shaped Buddhist monument. Stupas were built to hold relics, such as the bones or belongings of the Buddha and other holy men.

TANG
The Tang dynasty ruled China from 618–907 CE.

TATTOOS
Pictures made on human skin by rubbing soot or other pigments into cuts.

TRADITION
Beliefs or behaviour passed on by people. Traditions can be passed on from one generation to another, or from people to people.

TREE RING DATING
Method of dating wood by the distinctive pattern of the annual growth rings of trees. These also help us learn about the climate in the past.

TRIBUTE
Wealth offered to powerful rulers by people they rule or have defeated in battle.

WET RICE FARMING
A method of growing rice in flooded fields.

ZIGGURAT
A stepped mud-brick temple found in Mesopotamia.

Index

A
Adena culture 69, 82, 83
Africa 4, 6, 22–31
  kingdoms 22, 28–29
  map 23
  sub-Saharan 22, 30–31
Alexander the Great 19, 32, 33, 40–41, 54
Americas 68–85
  map 69
Anasazi people 69, 84, 85
Angkor Wat 66, 67
Arabia 6, 20–21
Aristotle 39, 41
Ashoka the Great 55
Ashurbanipal, King 12–13
Asia 50–67
  map 51
Assyrian Empire 5, 6, 7, 12–13
astronomy 10, 74
Athens 38, 39
Augustus, Emperor 43
Australian Aborigines 86, 88–89
Axum 22, 23, 28, 29
Aztecs 68, 69, 71, 76–77

B
Babylonia 6, 7, 10–11
Baekje kingdom 51, 62, 63
ball courts 70, 72, 85
Bantu language 30
bedouin 20
Benin 22, 23, 30, 31
boats 21, 24, 90–91
Botta, Paul-Émile 13
Britain 34, 35, 46, 48
Bronze Age 32
Buddhism 55, 60, 61, 62, 63, 65, 66
building 4–5, 44, 47, 53, 81, 85

C, D
Caesar, Julius 43, 49
Cahokia 83
Canaan 6, 14–15
Carnac, France 35
Carthage 16, 17, 42
cedar forests 16
Celtic tribes 32, 48–49
Champa kingdom 51, 66
Chang'an 60–61, 63, 64, 65
Chavín culture 69, 78
Chichén Itzá 74
China 46, 50, 51, 58–61, 64
Christianity 28, 29, 47
Circus Maximus 44
cities 6, 7
civilizations 4–5
Colosseum 45
conquistadors 77, 81
Constantine, Emperor 47
Corinth 42
Cortés, Hernán 77
Crete 36–37, 39
cuneiform 5, 8, 9
Darius the Great 18–19
deserts 20, 28, 88

E, F
Easter Island 92
Egypt 5, 14, 20, 22, 23, 24–27, 28, 29, 41
Etruscans 42
Euphrates, river 8, 10
Europe 32–49
  map 33
Evans, Sir Arthur 37
farming 4, 5, 25, 28, 30, 47, 65, 73, 76, 81, 83, 84, 85, 91
flint mining 35

G, H
Garamantes 22, 23, 28
Ghana 22, 23, 30, 31
gold 31, 37, 56, 63
Greece
Classical 18, 32, 33, 38–39
Mycenaeans 32, 36–37
resistance to Rome 42
Gupta Empire 51, 54, 55
Hadrian's Wall 46
Hammurabi, King 10–11
Han Empire 51, 60, 62
Hellenistic Age 40, 41
hieroglyphs 5, 25
hill forts 48
Hinduism 54, 66, 67
Hittite Empire 7, 14
Hohokam people 69, 84, 85
Hopewell tradition 69, 82, 83
hoplites 39
Huns 57
hunter-gatherers 4
hunting 12–13, 88

I, J, K
Incas 68, 69, 80–81
incense 20–21
India 21, 29, 41, 46, 50, 52
  empires 50, 51, 54–55
Indus Valley 50, 51, 52–53
Islam 21
Israelites (Jews) 6, 11, 15
jade 71
Japan 50, 64–65
Jerusalem 11, 15
Kaya 63
Khmer Empire 51, 66
Khufu, Pharaoh 26, 27
kings 5
Knossos 36, 37
Koguryo kingdom 51, 62
Korea 50, 62–63, 64

L, M
Layard, Austen Henry 13
Lebanon 16
Machu Picchu 81
Ma'rib 20, 21
mathematics 55, 74
Mauryan Empire 51, 54–55
Maya 68, 69, 72–75
Mediterranean 6, 16, 46
megaliths 34–35
Melanesia 86, 87, 92
Meroë 22, 23, 28, 29
Mesoamerica, early 68, 70–71
Mesopotamia 5, 8, 12, 46
metals 6, 8, 22, 29, 30, 31, 48, 63
Mexico 71, 76–77
Micronesia 87, 90, 92
Middle East 6–21
  map 7
Minoans 32, 36–37
Mississippi culture 69, 82, 83
Moche people 69, 79
Mogollon 69, 84, 85
Mohenjo-Daro 52–53
monument builders 32, 34–35
mound builders 68, 82–83
mummies 26, 80
music 4, 14, 89
Mycenaeans 32, 36–37

N, O
Nabataea 7, 21
Nabonidus, King 11
Nan Madol 92, 93
Nazca 69, 78, 79
Nebuchadnezzar, King 10, 11
Neolithic Age 32, 34–35
Nero, Emperor 43
New Zealand Maori 91, 92
Newgrange, Ireland 34
Nile, river 24–25
Nineveh 12–13
Nok 23, 30
North America 82–85
Nubia 28, 29
Olmecs 69, 70
Olympic Games 39

P, Q
Pacific peoples 86, 87, 90–93
Pagan Kingdom 51, 66
Pakal, King 74, 75
Paracas people 78
Pergamum 41
Pericles 38
Persepolis 18, 19, 40
Persian Empire 6, 7, 18–19, 40
Persian Wars 18, 39
Peru 78, 80–81
Petra 21
pharaohs 5, 25, 26
Philip II, king of Macedon 40
Philistines 6, 14–15
Phoenicians 6, 7, 16–17
Pizarro, Francisco 81
Pohnpei 92, 93
Polynesia 86, 87, 90–91, 92
printing 61
pueblo farmers 68, 84–85
pyramids 26, 29, 71, 72, 75, 76–7
  Great Pyramid of Giza 26, 27
Qur'an 21

R, S
religion 5, 11, 13, 14, 17, 18, 25, 47, 49, 61, 71, 74, 77, 89
  goddess 37, 64
  see also specific faiths
roads 18, 46, 58
Roman Empire 28, 32, 33, 42–43, 46–47, 49
Rome, City of 32, 42, 44–45
sacrifice 17, 63, 70, 73, 76, 77, 91
Scythians 51, 57
shamanism 57, 62
Shi Huangdi 58
Shinto 65
Sicily 39
Silk Road 60
Silla kingdom 51, 63
Skara Brae, Orkney 34
Solomon, King 15
South America 68, 78–79
Southeast Asia 66–67
Sparta 38, 39
Srivijaya Empire 51, 66
standing stones 35
stelae 29
Steppe Nomads 50, 56–57
Stonehenge 35
Sumer 6, 8–9

T, U, V
taboos 92
Tang dynasty 51, 60–61, 62, 63
tattoos 57, 92
Temple of the Inscriptions 74, 75
Tenochtitlán 76–77
Teotihuacán 71
Terracotta Army 59
Thera (Santorini) 36
Tigris, river 8, 12
Tikal 72
Tiwanaku 69, 78–79
Toltecs 71
tombs 26, 34, 56, 59, 62, 63, 64, 75, 82–83
trade 9, 16, 21, 22, 29, 36, 46, 53, 60, 62
Trajan, Emperor 46
Tyre 16, 17
Ur 4–5, 8–9
Vandals 47
Vercingetorix 49

W, Z
warfare 5, 8, 13, 40–41, 43, 49, 61, 73, 83
wheels 9, 58, 79
writing 5, 8, 9, 17, 21, 25, 37, 53, 59, 70, 74
Wu Zetian 61
Xerxes, King 18, 19
Yamato dynasty 64–65
Zapotecs 69, 70
ziggurats 4–5, 8–9
Zimbabwe, Great 22, 23, 30, 31

Credits

The publisher would like to thank the following for their kind permission to reproduce their photographs:
Abbreviations key: a-above, b-below/bottom, c-centre, l-left, r-right, t-top

akg-images: 4c, 13tr, 14c, 15tl, 49b, 52bl, 56c; Peter Connolly 40–41tc; Mark De Fraeye 56-57tc; Andrea Jemolo 26br; Erich Lessing 6bl, 13tl, 18tr, 42bl, 47tr, 48c; RIA Novosti 57tc; **Alamy Images**: AEP 44c; Auscape International Pty Ltd 86br, 88–89b; B&Y Photography 43cr; David Ball 50bc, 63b; Suzy Bennett 89tl; Anders Blomqvist 55tc; Victor Paul Borg 28cr; Sylvia Cordaiy Photo Library Ltd 66c; Deco Images 32tc, 44br; Ros Drinkwater 34b; Stephen Finn 47tl; TH Foto 28b; © gezmen 56-57b; Hemis 35cr; Peter Horree 73bc; Chris Howes/Wild Places Photography 31t; INTERFOTO Pressebildagentur 8cl; ITB Photo Communications, Inc 14tl, 17b; Richard Levine 85tl; The London Art Archive 10c, 49tl; Mary Evans Picture Library 13c, 41cr; Neil McAllister 50br, 66bc; MJ Photography 54-55b; Geoffrey Morgan 59cr; Richard Osbourne/Blue Pearl Photographic 39c; David Paterson 21tl; Picture Contact 29tc; Nicholas Pitt 84–85bc; The Print Collector 44tr; An Qi 61t; Robert Harding Picture Library Ltd 6cr, 10–11; Mireille Vautier 74br; Ken Welsh 72b; Ariadne Van Zandbergen 29r; **Ancient Art & Architecture Collection**: 32cra, 47bl, 63tr; **The Art Archive**: Archaeological Museum Cividale Friuli/Alfredo Dagli Orti 11tr; Archaeological Museum Lima/Gianni Dagli Orti 80bl; Biblioteca Nacional Madrid/Gianni Dagli Orti 77bl; Bodleian Library Oxford 76br; British Library 50bl, 58tc, 61c; British Museum/Gianni Dagli Orti 5tr; Gianni Dagli Orti 6tr, 14br, 15bl, 18bl, 77tc; Musée du Louvre Paris/Gianni Dagli Orti 9tc, 13cr; Museo di Villa Giulia Rome/Gianni Dagli Orti 39tl; National Archaeological Museum Athens/Gianni Dagli Orti 36bl; Alfredo Dagli Orti 58bl; Antiquarium di Santa Severa/Alfredo Dagli Orti 17tc; Staatliche Glyptothek Munich/Alfredo Dagli Orti 43br; Victoria and Albert Museum London/Eileen Tweedy 64cl; Jean Vinchon Numismatist Paris/Gianni Dagli Orti 47br; **The Bridgeman Art Library**: Brooklyn Museum of Art, New York, USA 80bc; Museo e Gallerie Nazionali di Capodimonte, Naples, Italy 43cl; Private Collection 21cl; **The Trustees of the British Museum**: 6cl, 8bl, 9tr, 10, 11br, 12–13b, 22tl, 29c, 90bl; Corbis: 15tr, 40-41b; The Art Archive 47c, 77br; David Ball 46cr; Bettmann 81tr; Christophe Boisvieux 78–79b; Richard A Cooke 85br; Owen Franken 12cl; Chris Hellier 37tl; Hulton-Deutsch Collection 37br; Jon Arnold/JAI 24-25b; Kimbell Art Museum 92cl; Korea News Service 62br; Ludo Kuipers 88cl; Charles & Josette Lenars 55cr, 73t, 78t; Michael S Lewis 82-83b; Araldo de Luca 32tl; Maurice Nimmo/Frank Lane Picture Agency 35bl; Kazuyoshi Nomachi 21tr; Richard T Nowitz 41br; Alfredo Dagli Orti 25cc; Gianni Dagli Orti 40bl, 76bl; Ruggero Vanni 13br; Sandro Vannini 46b; Michael Y Yamashita 4–5b; **Peter Crawford**: 86tl, 90–91; **DK Images**: 37tc; Max Alexander 36–37b; Max Alexander/Archaeological Receipts Fund (TAP) 37tr; The British Museum 38bl; Nigel Hicks 38br; Alan Hills, The British Museum 49tr; Chas Howson/The British Museum 41tr; J Kershaw/The British Museum 55tr; Jamie Marshall 72cr; National Museum, New Delhi 53tc; Karl Shone/Courtesy of the Ermine Street Guard 43tl; Michel Zabe/CONACULTA-INAH-MEX 77br; **Getty Images**: Michael J P Scott 68cac; Stone/ Michael J P Scott 81bc; Yoichi Tsukioka 50tr, 64bl; **Mary Evans Picture Library**: 57cr; **Courtesy of Leonard Pole**: 30cl; **Robert Harding Picture Library**: Jochen Schlenker 6cr; **Royal Ontario Museum**: 59tr; **Photo Scala, Florence**: Musée du Quai Branly, Paris 30cr; **TopFoto. co.uk**: AAAC 62bl; **Werner Forman Archive**: Arizona State Museum 84bl; British Museum, London 92bc; Edgar Knobloch 52–53bc; Museum of the American Indian, Heye Foundation, New York 83tl; Ohio State Museum 69tr; San Francisco Museum of Asiatic Art 63tl; Smithsonian Institution, Washington 83cr; Sudan Archaeological Museum, Khartoum 29tl; Euan Wingfield 18br; **West Virginia Division of Culture and History**: 82c.

Jacket images: Front: **Alamy Images**, Image Gap c; **Getty Images**: Stone/Michael J P Scott br; **Photolibrary**: Corbis fbl; **Werner Forman Archive**: British Museum, London fbr; Ninja Museum, Uemo bl. Back: **Corbis**: Roger Ressmeyer. Spine: **Alamy Images**: Art Kowalsky.

All other images © Dorling Kindersley
For further information see: www.dkimages.com

The publisher would also like to thank Charlotte Webb for proofreading, Jackie Brind for the index, and Sunita Gahir and Bulent Yusuf for the CD creation.